THE FANTASY SPORTS BOSS 2017 NFL DRAFT GUIDE

BY MICHAEL E. KENESKI

TABLE OF CONTENTS

1. Editor's Note…………………………………………..……..Page 3
2. 2017 NFL Draft Ten Burning Questions…………………Page 4
3. 2017 NFL Mock Draft……………………………………Page 7
4. 2017 NFL Draft Team-By-Team Needs……………..Page 11
5. 2017 NFL Draft Position Rankings & Scouting Reports….Page 16
    - Quarterbacks……………………………………………Page 16
    - Running Backs…………………………………….Page 24
    - Fullback………………………………………….Page 32
    - Wide Receivers……………………………………..Page 33
    - Tight Ends………………………………………….Page 45
    - Offensive Tackles………………………………….Page 51
    - Centers………………………………………….....Page 58
    - Guard…………………………………………….Page 61
    - Kicker/Punter/Long Snapper…………………….Page 66
    - Defensive End…………………………………….Page 67
    - Defensive Tackle………………………………….Page 74
    - Outside Linebacker……………………………….Page 81
    - Middle Linebacker……………………………….Page 88
    - Strong Safety…………………………………….Page 92
    - Free Safety……………………………………….Page 97
    - Cornerback……………………………………….Page 101
6. Round 1 Log………………………………………...Page 110

Editor's Note

Once the final play of the Super Bowl is in the books, there is a feeling of depression or sadness for all fans of the NFL. While the Super Bowl is the highlight of the football season, all but the fans of the two last teams standing have begun their hibernation from the sport that lasts from the start of February all the way to the opening of training camps in mid-July. The five months spanning those two NFL calendar points can seem like an endless slog or like a barren desert of nothing but non-football sporting events. Luckily there is a three-day oasis to help with the NFL withdrawals which of course is the annual extravaganza that is the draft. Few events draw such maddening attention and excitement (along with quizzical looks from those non-NFL fans who can't fathom why anyone would watch a scrolling ticker of names for three days) than the selection of the top collegiate pros by the 30 teams from around the league. The draft has become must-see TV even for casual fans of the sport as the players selected during the proceedings represent hope for the future. So it is with that backdrop that we once again bring you the Fantasy Sports Boss 2017 NFL Draft Guide which is jam-packed with hundreds of profiles and analysis from every position on the field. Our staff have pored over literally thousands of hours and hundreds of games worth of tape on these players and our reports indicate where we think each of them stand in terms of their professional outlook. While we don't profess to be right on every one of these players, we do feel strongly that the trends on their tape spell out how they will adapt once at the next level. So sit back with the guide and enjoy this strange but yet exciting bit of Americana.

Yours truly,

Michael E. Keneski

The Fantasy Sports Boss

2017 NFL DRAFT TEN BURNING QUESTIONS

Questions, questions, and more questions. It wouldn't be the NFL Draft if there weren't an abundance of them. With the draft being nothing but a cross your fingers and hope for the best exercise, any bit of information to try and cut through the murkiness is always appreciated. With that in mind, we compiled ten questions and answers on what we think are prime issues heading into the draft. While they won't go anywhere near clearing up the massive confusion and anxieties that accompany any draft, we at least hope this shapes some of the storyline.

1. Q: So let's go right to the top in asking who will the Cleveland Browns (or the future team they could trade the pick to) be taking number 1 overall at the 2017 NFL Draft?

A: The Browns are always a major wild card at the draft and so trying to nail down who they will take is like throwing darts against a wall of names. They are clearly in need of a franchise QB but taking Mitch Trubisky number 1 is a bit of a reach since he is not considered to be the type of passing prospect worth going that high. That leaves the two clear-cut top prospects that both come from the defensive end position in the form of Alabama's Jonathan Allen and Texas A@M's Myles Garrett. Garrett was considered the clear-cut pick for months but Allen is getting late play but either way both guys are ferocious pass rushers who will be instant stars at the NFL level. The consensus seems to be that Garrett has more upside than Allen and so he would be our pick for number 1 overall.

2. Q: since you mentioned Trubisky, who could join the strong-armed Tar Hell as first round passers?

A: This is not considered to be an especially strong quarterback class this season but be that as it may, QB-needy teams never waste much time addressing this very important position in Round 1. That means Trubisky should be joined by Clemson's DeShaun Watson and Notre Dame's DeShon Kizer as first round picks and while all three have impressive talent, they all also carry question marks (Trubisky's poor footwork in pocket, Watson's and Kizer's label of being more athlete than passer). Also keep an eye on Texas A@M's Patrick Mahomes who is quickly rising up draft boards.

3. Q: The running back position is making a comeback in terms of early-round importance given the incredible rookie season of Ezekiel Elliott in 2016. That should portend to good things for Dalvin Cook and Leonard Fournette right?

A: Cook looks like the next Le'Veon Bell as a monster talent in both the running and receiving game which should net him a top ten pick easy. Meanwhile Fournette is not as universally liked as many fear his big body and penchant for getting injured are big red flags for the next level. Then there is Stanford's Christian McCaffrey who set all sorts of offensive records for the Cardinal. Now while there is doubt that McCaffrey can hold up as a bellcow back at the NFL level but a Randall Cobb-like role where he helps on both sides of the offensive attack should allow him to go in Round 1 as well.

4. Q: Where does the positional strength lie in the 2017 NFL Draft?

A: Offensive tackle, running back, wide receiver, defensive end, and cornerback look well-stocked this season. Also while not as potent as in years past, defensive tackle still has a decent amount of talent among its class.

5. Q: On the flip side, at what positions is talent lacking?

A: Center, both safety spots, inside linebacker, and tight end are not especially strong or deep in talent this season. Quarterback is shallower than in years past as well.

6. Q: Which potential first-round picks carry the most bust risk?

A: There is no exact science to figuring out who the next "bust pick" will be since if that were the case, these players would be avoided by all. Since we don't have psychic abilities, what we can do is look at players who have some characteristics at their position that have led to bust seasons for earlier prospects. Right away DeShaun Watson stands out due to his physical similarities to Robert Griffin III who of course became a big bust after initially excelling as a rookie. Both Griffin and Watson have slight builds and also had accuracy question marks coming out of college. We also have issues with Leonard Fournette as a big back who has been banged up a lot in college. Bigger backs like Fournette tend to take more of a pounding from NFL defenders and that could lead to more injuries and a shorter professional shelf life like what we saw out of Jamaal Anderson, Larry Johnson, and Eddie George. Finally, USC wideout JuJu Johnson has speed issues that could make it tough for him to separate against NFL corners like we saw from Laquan

Treadwell in his 2016 debut. Also keep in mind USC has a recent horrible track record of sending wideouts to the NFL as Dwayne Jarrett and Mike Williams were huge busts.

7. Q: Talk about some potential first round gems that could go in the middle-to-late portion of the round?

A: While he was severely underutilized in the Alabama passing attack, tight end O.J. Howard looks like a star-in-the-making. Howard has off-the-charts athleticism for the position and he possesses the receiving ability to become a Pro Bowler very quickly. Also while DeShon Kizer, DeShaun Watson, and Mitch Trubisky get most of the first-round QB attention, don't sleep on Texas A@M's Patrick Mahomes who has tremendous natural tools that include a cannon for an arm and solid accuracy. It would not be a shock if Mahomes ended up being the best QB in the 2017 class.

8. Q: Is Ohio State's Malik Hooker the next Ed Reed or Sean Taylor?

A: Very rarely do you see a safety get picked within the first ten selections of the NFL Draft but that will surely happen this time around as the Buckeyes' Hooker is just that talented to go so high. While Reed was drafted 24th overall by the Baltimore Ravens, Taylor went fifth overall to the Washington Redskins. Hooker could be in play right around the same spot as Taylor as the San Diego Chargers at 6 are very interested and have a big need there. Hooker certainly checks all the boxes as a big-hitter who is also excellent in coverage. He won't last long.

9. Q: Alabama's entire team seems like they will get drafted in 2017 huh?

A: We all knew that Nick Saban built a dynasty at Alabama but at the same time, he also has crafted an unmatched conveyer belt of prospects that head to the pro ranks on a yearly basis. 2017 might take things to a whole new extreme there as Alabama could easily see more than 15 players drafted, with a ridiculous 6 going in Round 1. Making things even more absurd is that even their specialists (kicker, punter, and long snapper) stand a good chance of being picked in the late rounds.

10. Q: Teez Taylor or Marlon Humphrey as the best cornerback in the draft?

A: These two are so evenly matched that you can pretty much flip a coin between them. Both can cover and are supremely athletic but Taylor has some off-the-field issues which include two team suspensions from Florida that tilt things in Humphrey's direction.

NFL MOCK DRAFT

While our attempts to figure out the first round of the 2017 NFL Draft was as scientific as we could possibly make it, we all know the carnage that will surely take place among the first 32 picks will likely change the outlook here dramatically. Still we gave it our best shot so here it goes:

1. Cleveland Browns-Myles Garrett (DE, Texas A@M): You Browns may think about Mitch Trubisky or DeShaun Watson for a second or two but neither is considered worthy of being a number 1 overall QB pick like a Peyton Manning or an Andrew Luck. Hopefully for their sake the Browns take the pass-rushing monster that is Texas A@M's Myles Garrett who is the best player in the draft.

2. San Francisco 49ers-Mitch Trubisky (QB, North Carolina): The 49ers are desperate for a quarterback and they won't want another run-pass guy like Watson after finishing up with the ugly Colin Kaepernick years.

3. Chicago Bears-Jonathan Allen (DE, Alabama): While the Bears have their own quarterback problems, head coach John Fox always leans defense which guides him to taking Alabama's Jonathan Allen who some think could go first overall instead of Myles Garrett.

4. Jacksonville Jaguars-Dalvin Cook (RB, Florida State): Neither Chris Ivory nor T.J. Yeldon is the answer at running back for the Jags who have been looking for a prime player there seemingly since the days of Fred Taylor. Cook looks like a Le'Veon Bell clone who can add big-play capabilities both in the receiving and running game and also bring in some Florida State fans.

5. Tennessee Titans-Jamal Adams (SS, LSU): There could be two safeties go in the top ten picks which is very rare to see, starting with LSU's Adams who fills a gigantic need for the sieve-like Tennessee secondary.

6. New York Jets-Marshon Lattimore (CB, Ohio State): Anyone who saw how terrible and clearly washed-up Darrell Revis was last season would fully understand this pick. Lattimore can be one of the next great cover guys in the NFL and he is more than qualified taking the torch from Revis.

7. Los Angeles Chargers-Malik Hooker (FS, Ohio State): Yet another safety going this early as the hard-hitting Hooker can help address a big need for the Chargers ever since Eric Weddle departed.

8. Carolina Panthers-Cam Robinson (OT, Alabama): All you need to see is how often Cam Newton got lit up behind a suddenly leaky Carolina offensive line to realize Robinson has to be the guy in this spot.

9. Cincinnati Bengals-Reuben Foster (LB, Alabama): The Bengals have the offensive pieces down pat but the defense needs an overhaul after they got mauled all too often. This Alabama tackling machine instantly becomes one of the most impactful players on that side of the ball.

10. Buffalo Bills-Mike Williams (WR, Clemson): With Rex Ryan and his defensive draft leanings out of town, the Bills finally give themselves insurance for the inevitable next Sammy Watkins injury.

11. New Orleans Saints-Tim Williams (LB, Alabama): The Saints could go in any direction on defense but this pass rushing linebacker will do just fine.

12. Cleveland Browns-DeShaun Watson (QB, Clemson): I think Watson will fall here as his accuracy is shaky and the comparisons to RGIII will scare some teams off. Leave it to the Browns to take Watson just a year after starting Griffin.

13. Arizona Cardinals-Curtis Samuel (WR, Ohio State): With Larry Fitzgerald possibly retired by the time you read this and Michael Floyd having been cast aside, Samuel makes total sense here.

14. Indianapolis Colts-Leonard Fournette (RB, LSU): Yes they always need offensive linemen but Fournette is a good pick here to replace the ancient Frank Gore.

15. Philadelphia Eagles-John Ross III (WR, Washington): The Eagles need to surround QB Carson Wentz with some more receiving talent and this big-play guy can surely fit the bill there.

16. Baltimore Ravens-Derek Barnett (DE, Tennessee): With Terrell Suggs really starting to get up there in age, the Ravens need to overhaul the pass rush.

17. Washington Redskins-Solomon Thomas (DE, Stanford): The Redskins would have been a decent contender to make the Super Bowl last season if their defense were merely adequate and not the complete train wreck they were last season. This fine-tuned defensive end will go a long way toward remedying that giant shortcoming.

18. Tennessee Titans-Corey Davis (WR, Western Michigan): It was criminal how few weapons the Titans supplied emerging QB Marcus Mariota last season. While Davis comes from a small school, he was a pass catching machine for Western Michigan.

19. Tampa Bay Buccaneers-Tampa Bay Buccaneers-Teez Tabor (CB, Florida): The Bucs are in the same division as passing game stars Drew Brees and Matt Ryan so shoring up their secondary is a tremendous need.

20. Denver Broncos-Ryan Ramczyk (OT, Wisconsin): The offensive line performed poorly for the Broncos last season and that was especially true out wide. Wisconsin has a great tradition of sending top-notch blockers to the NFL and Ramczyk seems set to join that hallowed fraternity.

21. Detroit Lions-Malik McDowell (DT, Michigan State): The Lions have been looking for a prime run-stuffer since losing Ndamakung Suh and McDowell has the beef and power to start clogging up lanes immediately.

22. Miami Dolphins-O.J. Howard (TE, Alabama): This one makes too much sense not to happen as the Dolphins have had some of the worst tight end receiving production in the game over the last five seasons.

23. New York Giants-Garrett Boles (OT, Utah): With the Giants realizing that Ereck Flowers is not suitable for left tackle, they get right to work finding a new blind side protector for the aging Eli Manning.

24. Oakland Raiders-Sidney Jones (CB, Washington): The biggest issue the Raiders had last season was a secondary that got torched on a weekly basis. Enter this hard-hitting cover guy and Jones will quickly shore up that weakness.

25. Houston Texans-Jabril Peppers (S, Michigan): The Texans also need help in their secondary to complement the tremendous pass rush they have up front.

26. Seattle Seahawks-Dan Feeney (G, Indiana): While they wanted one of the three top tackles that went prior to this pick, the Seahawks go into the guard tier to grab this potent blocker from Indiana to help cure what was a comically inept unit across the board last season.

27. Kansas City Chiefs-Marlon Humphrey (CB, Alabama): The secondary for the Chiefs is getting a bit worn and failed to support the team's very good pass rush last season. Humphrey is a confident corner who comes from the most successful college program in the country to help in that area.

28. Dallas Cowboys-Charles Harris (DE, Missouri): The Cowboys could go wide receiver here but we think they will lean on this solid all-around end to help prevent another Aaron Rodgers 2016 playoff assault in 2017.

29. Green Bay Packers-Quincy Wilson (CB, Florida): By the end of the Packers' playoff run last season, they virtually had nobody left to man the secondary. A much-needed infusion of youth here.

30. Pittsburgh Steelers-Takkharist McKinley (LB, UCLA): The great Steelers defenses of recent memory were filled with ferocious linebackers such as Kevin Greene, Greg Lloyd, James Farrior, James Harrison, and Joey Porter and that makes the underwhelming units they have used the last few seasons that much more noticeable in terms of needing a change.

31. Atlanta Falcons-Carl Lawson (DE, Auburn): The Falcons have the offense down pat and so now they need to get a pass rushing complement to Vic Beasley.

32. New England Patriots-Christian McCaffrey (RB, Stanford): Bill Belichick will have a field day using this running/receiving weapon all over the field.

2017 NFL DRAFT TEAM NEEDS

There is no such thing as an NFL team that has zero needs. Even the perennially dominant New England Patriots have holes which need to be filled (and quite a bit if you ever listen to the always unsatisfied Bill Belichick) and that is where the NFL Draft comes into play. While free agency can solve some short-term needs, the NFL draft has been proven to be the best method for re-stocking the roster shelves both for the present and well into the future. So with that said, let's take a closer look at the team needs for all 30 NFL outfits in terms of the positions they will be giving extra focus to this April.

Arizona Cardinals (QB, WR, OG, OT): Carson Palmer is on fumes and Larry Fitzgerald might already be retired by the time you read this. Also at wideout, Michael Floyd was cut loose and John Brown took a major step back in 2016. The line didn't help matters either and in particular the guard play was terrible.

Atlanta Falcons (CB, DE, DT): The Falcons' secondary has been a sieve for awhile and it stood out as a major weakness in the team's terrific 2016 season. While outside linebacker has become fortified with the development of Vic Beasley, the defensive line needs to get some more push.

Baltimore Ravens (WR, DE, CB, S): The Ravens just saw Steve Smith go off into retirement and Breshaud Perriman can't stay on the field at wideout. The defense has slipped badly the last two seasons as well, with a lacking pass rush that is depending on the aging Terrell Suggs being a sizable concern. The secondary also could use some weapons to combat Ben Roethlisberger and the potent Pittsburgh Steelers passing attack.

Buffalo Bills (QB, WR, CB, DT): The Bills have destroyed their relationship with the solid Tyrod Taylor and E.J. Manuel has been a joke every time he has taken snaps under center. A franchise QB is an absolute must for this team to gain some juice and hope for the future. They also look like a great landing spot for Clemson's Mike Williams who can serve as insurance for the next Sammy Watkins injury or future departure. While the defense played well for large stretches of last season, a corner opposite Stephon Gilmore would be a help and the run-stopping middle could use some reinforcements.

Carolina Panthers (OT, G, RB, S): An offensive tackle should be the top priority for the Panthers after seeing Cam Newton take hellacious hits all season long. An interior guard should be a close second to further address this pressing need. Also while Jonathan Stewart is a decent runner, he is aging and has never been very flashy or durable.

Chicago Bears (QB, CB, S, LB): The Bears have rightfully kicked Jay Cutler to the curb and anyone who saw how awful Matt Barkley played last season know the cupboard is bare at the most important position on the field for the team. Also ever since Lance Briggs went off into the sunset, the Bears have been looking for a new leader at linebacker. Finally, the secondary was horrendous all last season and could use help both at corner and safety.

Cincinnati Bengals (WR, LB, DE, OT): The defense needs pass-rushing help as that aspect of the unit has really slipped lately. The offensive line gave up the second most sacks in the league in 2016 and star tackle Andrew Whitworth is not getting any younger. Also when A.J. Green went down, there was no wideout to step up in his place.

Cleveland Browns (QB, RB, OT): The Browns seriously need to address the offense which is lacking in playmakers, blockers, and a franchise QB. After passing on Carson Wentz at the top of last year's draft, the Browns needs to come away with a passer they can groom to be a potential ten-year starter. The offensive line needs helps as well and that is especially true at the tackle spot. Finally, a speedy running back has been a need for awhile and that will help any quarterback they may draft.

Dallas Cowboys (TE, LB, DE): Jason Witten is still effective but he likely has just a year or two left. On the defensive side, the Cowboys have failed miserably in trying to find a pass-rushing complement for DeMarcus Lawrence. The linebacker corps has been up-and-down as well.

Denver Broncos (LB, G, OT, TE): Trevor Siemian was under duress for most of the 2016 season as the aging and ineffective Denver offensive line graded out as one of the worst units in the league. A pass-catching tight end has been a need since Julius Thomas left as a free agent. Also some better run-stopping linebacker help would be a nice bonus to go with the team's massive pass rush.

Detroit Lions (RB, OT, LB): The Lions have had to address the offensive line for a few years now as Matthew Stafford remains under siege and suffered a broken finger late last season on a sack. A running back always seems to be a need since the Lions habitually use a ragtag committee. With the Lions having been destroyed on the ground towards the end of 2016, a run-stopping linebacker is a must.

Green Bay Packers (RB, G, CB, S): While the run defense was stout, the Packer secondary was a huge weak link on the 2016 team. Ty Montgomery was used as a pretty effective running back when Eddie Lacy got hurt but he is miscast there. With Lacy likely not being welcomed back, a three-down back could be a key part of the team's draft.

Indianapolis Colts (RB, OT, C, LB): Help along the offensive line is an annual plea from QB Andrew Luck and the Colts better do something ASAP or else they will continue to jeopardize their franchise passer. Frank Gore is older than dirt and so the Leonard Fournette-to-the-Colts seems like a good idea. The Colts also need to get more pressure from their linebacker unit which let them down last season.

Jacksonville Jaguars (RB, OT, CB, LB): Luke Joeckel has failed to turn into the franchise tackle the Jags thought they were getting and so a re-do is needed there. Chris Ivory and T.J. Yeldon both showed last season they can't stay healthy or adequately run the ball. Finally the defensive line finally seems filled with some talent but the linebacker unit and secondary need to come next.

Kansas City Chiefs (QB, DT, CB): The Chiefs can get after the passer but their run defense has really become an issue. Alex Smith is limited and aging which makes addressing quarterback another smart idea.

Los Angeles Chargers (QB, WR, OT): Philip Rivers is the same age as Eli Manning and so the Chargers need to get someone new in the pipeline at quarterback. Meanwhile the team's receiving corps was ravaged by injuries last season but even prior to that they were a collection of number 2's.

Los Angeles Rams (WR, OT, C, CB): The Rams really need to begin surrounding QB Jared Goff with some receiving and blocking talent or he will go down as the huge bust he already is starting to look like based on his 2016 results. The secondary was picked apart for most of 2016 as well and this unit needs to get more in line with the team's impressive pass rush.

Miami Dolphins (G, DT, LB): The interior of the Miami line has become a weak point and needs a boost. While the defense generates good pass rushing heat, the run defense was below-average last season.

Minnesota Vikings (RB, QB, OT): The Vikings had arguably the worst offensive line in football last season and two tackle picks are needed here to replace the awful Matt Khalil and Andrew Smith. No word on what condition Teddy Bridgewater will be in when he tries to come back next season and Sam Bradford is just a stopgap. Finally, Adrian Peterson looks like he is almost done and could be gone by the time you read this.

New Orleans Saints (LB, CB, G, QB): The linebacker unit for the Saints is simply brutal and they need help across the board there. Also Drew Brees is not getting any younger and a new franchise QB is beyond due.

New England Patriots (WR, OT, DE): The Pats could add some more pass rushing help after their defense really dominated last season. Also the wide receiver corps is constantly in a state of flux with injuries and free agency.

New York Giants (QB, OT, LB): GM Jerry Reese has already admitted that Eli Manning is in the decline phase of his career at the age of 36 and a so getting a high-ceiling prospect becomes a priority for the first time in what seems like forever. The Giants also need to move Erick Flowers out from left tackle where he was a turnstile at times last season and find somebody more capable early in the draft.

New York Jets (QB, CB, C, OT): The Jets need help all over, starting at QB where they royally whiffed on Christian Hackenberg in last year's draft. They also saw Darrelle Revis become one of the worst defensive backs football last season and the offensive line needs an infusion at tackle and center.

Oakland Raiders (CB, S, LB): The offense is just fine here and so attention needs to go toward the Raiders' brutal secondary which was torched all season long in 2016. Some help at linebacker is also something that needs to be front-and-center at the draft.

Philadelphia Eagles (WR, RB, DE): While Jordan Matthews is a decent receiver, he has not become the star the Eagles expected him to be. Help is needed there and also at running back where Ryan Mathews can't stay on the field and Darren Sproles is older than dirt.

Pittsburgh Steelers (DE, CB, LB): While the offensive line finally looks relatively stable for the first time in awhile, the defense continues to leak across the board. Some more pass rushing help at defensive end is key and the secondary remains inconsistent.

San Francisco 49ers (QB, WR, DE, DT): The 49ers are more in need of a QB than any other team and so this has to be priority number 1. The receiving corps was only slightly worse and has zero playmaking ability as currently constructed. A reconfiguration of the defensive line needs to be undertaken as well.

Seattle Seahawks (OT, G, CB): Russell Wilson has been running for his life for two seasons now as the offensive line is right there as one of the worst units in the league. While the overall defense remains potent, the cornerback position opposite Richard Sherman is a weak link.

Tampa Bay Buccaneers (DT, WR, OT): Jameis Winston could use another receiving weapon opposite Mike Evans and some better blocking would also be a help. The interior defensive line is beginning to age a bit and the run-stopping ability of the unit has eroded.

Tennessee Titans (G, TE, WR): The Titans really need to get some weapons for QB Marcus Mariota who had a huge breakout season in 2016 with very little to throw to. There is age among the team's tight ends and the receiving unit is as bad as any in the league.

Washington Redskins (WR, DE, DT): The Redskins defensive line has been a tremendous weakness for the team as they got little push last season and the run-stopping tendencies of the unit was poor. Also they could supply some more consistent receiver help for Kirk Cousins.

So there you have it. While these don't address all of the 30 respective teams' needs, it gives you a better idea as to what position they will at least target more heavily as the draft moves along.

2017 POSITION RANKINGS AND ANALYSIS

QUARTERBACK

Position Grade: B-

First Round Talent: DeShaun Watson, DeShon Kizer, Mitch Trubisky

Analysis: This is not a vintage quarterback class by any means; with nary a clear no-doubt franchise signal-caller like a Peyton Manning or an Andrew Luck. Still the position always has a few players who end up going in Round 1, as those organizations that are desperate for a quarterback feel the need to reach here more than at any other spot.

Mitch Trubisky (North Carolina): Should be the top quarterback taken as Trubisky is the better pure passer then DeShaun Watson and DeShon Kizer. While he doesn't possess anywhere near the athletic ability of those two, Trubisky has an NFL arm that can make all of the required throws. What stands out here is Trubisky's top-level accuracy and that is a much more important trait then pure arm strength as the former can't really be taught. Was very efficient for the Tar Heels throughout 2016 and was terrific in going through all of his reads upon the snap. Protected the football nicely which is another big plus. Tough kid who can take a hit. Stands in against the rush to deliver passes. Footwork in the pocket not overly impressive. Throws off his back foot a bit too much when the pocket breaks down. While he is not a burner by any means, Trubisky is capable of picking up yardage when he needs to run. Was surrounded by immense offensive talent at North Carolina which may lead to some questions about how good he really is. Also Trubisky has just one year of experience which is a sizable negative. Mark Sanchez also had just one year of experience at USC before becoming an NFL bust. The tools are evident however and that means Trubisky won't wait long to hear his name called.

NFL Comparison: Matt Ryan

DeShaun Watson (Clemson): As a college football player, Clemson's DeShaun Watson has few peers. Ultra-productive both running and passing the football,

Watson got the Tigers to the Final Four his last two years as a collegiate. Where he stands as an NFL prospect is a bit more of a mystery and that is now especially true as Watson comes off a 2016 campaign where he struggled with accuracy. Physically Watson is not built the way you want your franchise QB to look which is a big concern. Barely standing over 6-0 and at a lanky 215 pounds, Watson will likely struggle with injuries unless he bulks up. A comparison to Robert Griffin III is pretty accurate as both guys were on the smallish side physically and in the case of Griffin, NFL pounding derailed his pro career quickly. Throws over 40 yards were noticeably an issue and overall Watson's accuracy is a concern. Also there are system concerns here as well since Watson didn't work in an NFL-type offense which inflated his numbers. On the plus side, Watson has speed to burn and can run like the wind. Keeps the play alive by quickly escaping the pocket and putting defenses on their toes. Clutch player who doesn't lose his head when the game is tight which is a big plus. Calm under pressure who steps up in big moments. Could go either way.

NFL Comparison: Robert Griffin III

DeShon Kizer (Notre Dame): Physically Kizer might be the most talented quarterback in the 2017 NFL Draft. Shows excellent vision and very good feet in the pocket to keep the play alive. Puts the football where a receiver can keep stride and continue moving down the field. Arm strength terrific to where Kizer can make all the throws. Accuracy good but not great. Misses some easy ones from time to time. Throwing mechanics can use some work. Has the speed to tuck it and run. There is a lot to work with here but Kizer needs to show he wants to put the work in to succeed.

Davis Webb (Cal): Spread system QB who put up very impressive numbers for Texas Tech and later Cal. Has a nice combination of size and accuracy. Webb also possesses a very good arm but not a pure cannon. Accuracy wanes past 50 yards in a noticeable way. Rough around the edges in terms of being a pocket passer. Doesn't always go through his reads and often locks in onto his receiver which an NFL secondary will go to town on. The biggest reservation some will have about Webb was the awful rookie campaign of fellow Cal QB Jared Goff. Goff too came from a spread system and was clueless in his 2016 debut when it came to diagnosing defenses and making reads.

*Pat Mahomes (Texas Tech): First let's get the obvious out of the way in stating there is no denying that "Air Raid" quarterbacks have been a huge flop in the NFL.

However Mahomes has physical traits and tools that most other previous Air Raid QB's did not possess such as an NFL arm and very good accuracy. Mahomes can make almost all the throws and his ball placement is excellent. Where Mahomes does need work is in his pocket skills. All too often Mahomes danced around in the pocket and his setup was not very good consistent in terms of properly releasing the football. Needs to step into his throws more. Also a big red flag is the fact that Mahomes has a dreaded windup to his release which is the same issue that killed the NFL career of Byron Leftwich and has held back Brock Osweiler. Getting back to the plusses though, Mahomes is a terrific scrambler who keeps many plays alive. He is not looking to run when he gets out of the pocket but instead looks to make throws when escaping a rush like Russell Wilson does. Boom or bust kid but one worth developing for a year or two given the attributes.

Brad Kaaya (Miami): Project prospect all the way as Kaaya is a stationary passer who struggled badly in some big games for the Hurricanes throughout his collegiate career. While his arm grades out as above-average, Kaaya's mechanics go to hell when the pocket breaks down. He often stares down the rush and has happy feet when sensing pressure. What helps Kaaya (and keeps him as a person of interest) is his solid accuracy. When given the time to throw, Kaaya can place the football in tight windows and his placement is very good as well. Has a great deal of experience going back to 2014 which should speed up the learning curve. Worth an investment as a one-to-two season developmental player.

Nathan Peterman (Pittsburgh): What jumps out about Nathan Peterman is the fact the kid has guts. Peterman stands strong in the pocket and delivers strikes even when he knows he is about to get hit. Has the leadership "it" factor down pat and shows no fear on the field. Peterman possesses good feet and maneuverability in the pocket and he also can get out and pick up yardage when things break down. While he doesn't have the strongest arm, Peterman makes up for it with above-average accuracy. Not much of a winner while at Pitt but he led a pro-style offense that will speed up the learning curve. Someone will give him a chance and in a year or so Peterman could be ready to contribute.

*Jerod Evans (Virginia Tech) 6-2 238: Surprisingly came out early after just one year as the starter for the Hokies which always gives an evaluator pause. Evans certainly had the numbers to justify such a move though as he tossed 29 touchdown passes and ran for another 12 scores in 2016. He possesses a good frame and has underrated athleticism. Moves his feet well in the pocket to avoid the rush and keeps his eyes down the field. Can extend plays with his underrated agility as well. Locks onto his man a bit too much which will need to be fixed. Tends to throw off his back foot which causes the pass to lose momentum. Also Evans has too long of a passing windup which can be a big problem at the NFL level.

Chad Kelly (Mississippi): A torn ACL finished off the Rebels' Chad Kelly early in 2016 and his immediate outlook is a bit murky since he won't be recovered in time to perform at the Combine. Prior to the injury, Kelly once again showed himself to be a pure gun-slinger who thinks there is not a throw he can't make. Kelly's decision-making needs a lot of work as he tries to fit the football in windows that are not always there. Turnovers are an issue as a result of this approach and some coaches automatically throw out quarterbacks with this trait in believing they are too tough to coach. There is an NFL lineage here (and a very good one) as Kelly is the nephew of former Buffalo Bills star and Hall of Famer Jim Kelly. While his arm strength is very good, Kelly needs clear refinement before he takes the reins at the next level. Perhaps the most concerning issue with Kelly is his very long list of off-the-field trouble that includes a bar fight where he threatened to use a gun on a patron and also for getting involved with Clemson fans during a game. Major red flags here.

Josh Dobbs (Tennessee): Another spread system QB which makes projecting abilities difficult. Dobbs possesses good arm strength that can make most of the throws as he is at least impressive physically. The deep ball is not great but Dobbs has very good accuracy under 50 yards. Could function as a West Coast guy since Dobbs is very adept at completing crossing routes and curls……. Like the ball placement as well….. Has good speed and was a running threat for the Volunteers. Unfortunately Dobbs resorts to running at the first hint of trouble. He also seems very hesitant taking a hit and slight/lanky frame is a clear cause for concern. Decision-making in the pocket not terrific and Dobbs needs to step into his throws more. Really dislike the windup in Dobbs' throwing motion and he also shows an obvious hitch in his release that will be a problem if not corrected.

C.J. Beathard (Iowa): Beathard made the best of a tough situation as the QB of a Hawkeyes' offense that didn't give him much help both in terms of blocking and offensive talent. As always, you have to give extra points to a QB who comes from the NFL-type system run by head coach Kirk Ferentz. Beathard has terrific arm strength and better speed than you would think. Classic case of a guy whose game speed will be better than his actual 40-time at the Combine. What really is apparent is the toughness Beathard has as he took some hellacious hits behind the poor Iowa offensive line but kept on getting up. Played through injuries which counts for an extra something. What I don't like is that Beathard's accuracy is so-so and his work in the pocket grades out as nothing special. Locked onto his receiver way too much upon the snap and rarely went to a third read. Tends to sling the football as well instead of stepping into his throws but Beathard is an intriguing mid-round pick.

Cooper Rush (Central Michigan): Rush was a starter for three years at Central Michigan so he has seen a lot on the field which is a plus. Has a smooth flow to his release from center in transitioning to the backdrop. Like how Rush uses a slide step in the pocket to buy time and keep his eyes down the field. His mechanics fall to the wayside a bit though when sensing heat but Rush often stood tall in the pocket while delivering the football. Reads were not always on par as Rush threw behind his receivers too often. Needs to work on his ball placement and anticipation. Physically Rush has the size and strength to hold up to NFL hits and his arm is quite good. It also needs to be noted that Central Michigan had some horrible running games during Rush's tenure at the school, which made his passing numbers all the more impressive.

Alek Torgeson (Penn) 6-2 230 4.93: Ivy League QB prospect which brings to mind veteran NFL journeyman Ryan Fitzpatrick (a Harvard alumnus). Very productive player whose physical stature passes the NFL eye test. Torgeson has smooth passing mechanics and obviously is above-average in the intelligence department which will speed up the learning curve. Decent enough athleticism but not much of a runner. Scans the field well but needs to work on ball placement. Touch not great past 40 yards and doesn't have the gun to place the football in tight quarters. More of a system developmental player.

Zach Terrell (Western Michigan) 6-1 204 4.89: Stating the obvious, Terrell does not possess what most NFL personnel execs want physically in their QB draft prospers. Terrell is very slight in his build at just a shade over 200 pounds and he is barely 6-1 as well. Thus there is a big question mark concerning whether Terrell can sustain NFL pounding. He also has to overly rely on his speed to get out of the pocket and in the process find some passing lanes due to a lack of height. While those are very big issues, Terrell is a terrific overall athlete who makes up for a lack of a passing gun by showing tremendous accuracy. Moved the chains at a high clip at Western Michigan and Terrell protected the football nicely in not throwing many picks. Has to be drafted onto a West Coast team in order to have a realistic chance to stick however.

Tyler Stewart (Nevada): Collegiate career ended in a bad way as Stewart suffered a season-ending shoulder injury in October that required surgery. As far as Stewart's makeup, he displays solid accuracy up to 40 yards but then things begin to decline beyond that mark. Stewart also tends to hold onto the football too long to the point that he takes big hits like the one that knocked him out last season. Doesn't go through his reads as well as you would like and mobility just average. Strictly a late-round pick at best.

Mitch Leidner (Minnesota): Talented but severely unrefined passer. On a physical scale, Leidner makes the grade as his very strong arm can make all the throws and he can sling ropes into tight quarters. Love the build at 6-3 and 230. Footwork in the pocket is solid as well as Leidner shows a nice slide step to evade the rush. He also possesses impressive speed for someone Leidner's size; often picking up yardage when escaping the rush. Unfortunately Leidner has a lot to learn at the next level since he was used almost exclusively in the shotgun with the Gophers and his accuracy is a negative. Leidner is often late with his reads and as a result, ball placement is not good. Tends to stare down his target which leads to interceptions that will be a more pronounced struggle in the NFL. Has a foot surgery in his past but showed toughness paying behind a somewhat leaky Minnesota line.

Gunner Kiel (Cincinnati) 6-3 215 4.87: If you could be a journeyman college player, Gunner Kiel was it. Spent time at Indiana, had a commitment to LSU, and transferred to Cincy from Notre Dame. Very intriguing sleeper prospect as Kiel has a strong arm and his accuracy is tremendous. Showed an uncanny ability to put the ball where only his receiver could get it or placing it so that his target can maintain his stride. Also can get out and run or use his quickness to sidestep the rush and keep the play alive. Where he does run into trouble is not always going through his reads. Tends to lock in on his targets and also has happy feet when the rush gets close. Needs some more discipline in terms of patience when scanning the field but Kiel is a guy who should rise as the draft approaches.

Brady Gustafson (Montana): Some will compare him to Carson Wentz given the D-II level and 6-7 height but that is where the similarities end. Gustafson is a stationary pocket passer unlike Wentz and his slow delivery (which includes a windup) is always a big problem when making the jump to the NFL. Gustafson has a very good arm though and can take a pounding as he did at Montana. Highly intelligent kid who was lauded for work ethic. Will give himself a chance on that alone. Arm and build should at least get him an invite to camp.

Seth Russell (Baylor): Like with most recent Baylor quarterbacks, Seth Russell put up offensive numbers that jumped off the page given the spread system. That is when Russell was actually on the field as he dealt with some terrible injury luck while in college. A fractured vertebrae in his neck in 2015 was very scary but Russell made it back for the 2016 season. He was having a good but not great year (Russell struggled with accuracy) before suffering a gruesome broken left ankle in December that became a YouTube trending video. At 6-3 and 220, Russell physically can sling it but his accuracy was an issue (just 55 percent before the ankle break last season) and obviously his health is a major red flag. Unlikely to be drafted but could catch on as a free agent.

Sefo Liufau (Colorado) 6-3 230 4.76: Love the size and physical makeup here as Liufau is how you would draw up a potential NFL QB draft pick. A bit of a gun-slinger in college, Liufau has the arm strength to play that type of game since he can fit the football into tight windows and challenge down the field. Gets himself into trouble though with interceptions and Liufau has to really curb his tendency to stare down receivers. Decent feet in the pocket that buys Liufau more time and he also can get out and serve as a running threat. Dealt with injuries in college and accuracy not at the level you would like. Rough around the edges but well worth a late-round pick.

Bart Houston (Wisconsin) 6-3 235 4.93: Again late round picks when it comes to the QB position almost always include a prospect who has good size and arm strength as Wisconsin's Bart Houston has. While the Badgers don't have a good track record of sending quarterbacks to the next level, Houston will draw attention to his well-built frame and very impressive arm. There is a severe lack of athleticism here as Houston does not move well in the pocket and is prone to taking big hits due to his tendency to hold onto the football too long. Has backup appeal but lack of speed and fluidity limits the outlook.

Ryan Higgins (Louisiana Tech) 6-1 207 4.78: Athletic kid who overcomes lack of arm strength and build by completing a high percentage of passes. Higgins senses the rush nicely and keeps his feet moving to buy time when scanning the field. Like the ball placement here as Higgins is quite accurate with his throws but struggles begin when asked to throw beyond 40. Will go down right away when hit due to a lack of bulk and so protection was always key for Higgins while in school. Could provide a spark as a backup at the NFL level.

THE REST

Antonio Pipkin (Tiffin) 6-2 208 4.67

Wes Lunt (Illinois) 6-4 225 4.98

Sean Maguire (Florida State) 6-2 223 5.28

Aaron Bailey (Northern Iowa) 6-1 226 4.59

Trevor Knight (Texas A@M) 6-0 215 4.76

Garrett Fugate (Central Missouri State) 6-2 210 4.69

Austin Appelby (Florida) 6-4 240 5.09

Tommy Armstrong Jr. (Nebraska) 6-1 220 4.78

Nick Mullens (Southern Miss) 6-1 196 4.92

Philip Walker (Temple) 5-11 205 4.82

RUNNING BACK

Position Grade: A-

First Round Talent: Dalvin Cook, Leonard Fournette, Christian McCaffrey

Analysis: The comeback into the first round at the running back position remains in full swing as there are three obvious top-tier talents in Leonard Fournette, Dalvin Cook, and Christian McCaffrey. The depth is impressive here as well which makes running back one of the stronger positions in the draft.

Leonard Fournette (LSU) 6-1 230 4.45: Incredibly productive power back for the Tigers, Fournette led the nation in rushing yardage as a sophomore (1,953 yards and 22 scores on the ground). Unfortunately the encore fell way short in 2016 as Fournette battled injuries that kept him sidelined for a number of games. He is a tremendously powerful runner who can easily break away from tackles and keep churning forward. What makes Fournette special is that he also has the wiggle and speed to take things outside and open up yardage when he finds a seam. Love the patience here as Fournette waits for his blocking to open up holes and then has the burst to quickly exploit it. Coaches will love Fournette's above-average blocking ability. Shows no hesitancy to take on bigger defensive lineman in order to protect his QB. Shortcomings in the passing game are obvious. Hands not very impressive and that could take Fournette off the field at the next level on third downs. Durability also a major issue as Fournette dealt with a slew of injuries in his collegiate career. Needs to do a better job running with a lower center of gravity or else he will continue to take some big hits from NFL defenders which could lead to more injuries. Bigger backs like Fournette have gone bust at a decent clip at the NFL level over the years and that alone will give personnel execs pause.

NFL Comparison: LeGarrette Blount

Dalvin Cook (Florida State) 5-11 206 4.46: Love this kid. Would take Cook over Leonard Fournette every day of the week and twice on Sunday. Ready-made NFL starter from the jump, Cook set the all-time Florida State record for rushing yardage in blowing by Warrick Dunn (1,691 yards in 2015). Stardom was always in the cards for Cook who was a five-star recruit for the 'Noles. Cook has tremendous vision and the uncanny ability to quickly diagnose his blocking and identify the seams. Gets up the field with instant acceleration, which allows Cook to reel off huge chunks of yardage. Possesses great cutback ability and left many a defender grasping at air. Runs with a low and compact center of gravity and can take it to the house whenever an opening presents itself. Top-notch pass receiver out of the backfield, Cook will be a three-down back at the next level and likely will be a 50-catch guy right away. He does lack in size and strength however, with Cook often going down upon the first hit. Doesn't break many tackles when in tight and must rely on speed to make plays. Blocking is sketchy and needs a bunch of work. Should easily be a top ten pick and maybe top five.

NFL Comparison: Le'Veon Bell

Christian McCaffrey (Stanford) 6-0 200 4.48: Put up video-game numbers in college with the Cardinal. Good NFL genes being the son of former NFL wideout Ed McCaffrey. Literally did it all on the football field as McCaffrey was a huge weapon in the running, receiving, and return game. Crossed 2,000 rushing yards as a sophomore (2,019) and broke Barry Sanders' all-time record in all-purpose yardage in 2015. McCaffrey has a muscular frame and complements that with terrific speed and burst. Like with Dalvin Cook, McCaffrey's field vision is spectacular and he explodes through the hole in a flash. Football IQ is off-the-charts as McCaffrey is a great route-runner and always seems to be in the right spot. While he only carries 200 pounds, McCaffrey has good leg drive and surprising power that allowed him to break a high amount of tackles in college. There is not a better receiver among running backs in the entire draft as well and McCaffrey could be a 60-catch guy right away. Can also operate as a wideout if need be and contribute as a returner as a rookie. A bit concerning is the amount of work McCaffrey took on in college and that might have impacted him a bit in 2016 as his numbers fell. Also while McCaffrey has a strong frame, he is not built to be a bellcow back at the NFL level. His blocking is not good either despite McCaffrey showing a willingness to get his nose dirty. A Darren Sproles-like role awaits.

NFL Comparison: Darren Sproles

*Joe Mixon (Oklahoma) 6-1 226 4.48: Whichever NFL team drafts Joe Mixon should give their PR man an immediate raise given the controversy that will immediately erupt. Mixon of course was the player Oklahoma coach Bob Stoops suspended for all of the 2014 season after he punched a woman in the face at a deli. The video of the incident was released to the public this past December and the image was horrendous. Charged with misdemeanor assault and having to complete 100 hours of community service, Mixon is without a doubt the most polarizing player in the draft. After the NFL was embarrassed by the whole Ray Rice situation (another assault on a woman that was captured on video), Mixon's first round talent will likely fall at least a round and maybe more. Now in terms of ability, there is no denying the fact Mixon has tremendous skills since he is a gifted runner who also possesses impressive speed. Mixon shows eye-opening cutting and stop-on-a-dime ability. He also has the acceleration to score whenever and wherever he gets his hands on the ball. A true three-down back as Mixon has soft hands that pluck the football out of the air and he is a very good route runner. Outside of the off-the-field trouble, Mixon is loose with the football and fumbling was a problem with the Sooners. While his legs are quite strong, Mixon's upper body is lacking a bit in musculature which could lead to some injuries. The bottom line here is that Mixon has the talent but maybe not the character.

Jeremy McNichols (Boise State) 5-9 212 4.55: Looking to follow in the footsteps of former Boise State and current Miami Dolphins lead back Jay Ajayi. McNichols doesn't have the bulk and power of Ajayi but has much more shiftiness and speed. Junkyard dog runner who plays bigger than his smallish size, McNichols possesses good lower-body strength and leg drive. He also is a terrific pass catcher out of the backfield. On the negative side, McNichols can't block a lick which limits his usage some. McNichols ideally needs to operate in a timeshare given his physical shortcomings.

*Alvin Kamara (Tennessee) 5-10 215 4.55: Meet the new Jamaal Charles. Alvin Kamara comes out of school early with a light collegiate workload but some very impressive athletic visuals. Possessing tremendous burst and quick-twitch movement, Kamara is a threat to score whenever he touches the football. What sets Kamara apart from other running back prospects is his way above-average skills as a receiver. Kamara runs precise routes and snatches the football out of the air with soft hands. Will likely be used a returner as well given the speed and breakaway ability. Like with Charles though, Kamara could be on an NFL snap count as he is not overly big and muscular.

*D'Onta Foreman (Texas) 6-1 249 4.55: Doak Walker Award winner as the top running back in 2016 college football. It is not often you see a runner who is nearly 250 pounds but can run a sub-4.60 40 like Foreman can. Has a nose for the end zone as Foreman scored 15 touchdowns last season and averaged 6.3 per carry. Foreman is power personified as a runner, often running through defenders and falling forward with terrific upper-and-lower body strength. Overall Foreman is limited as he is a terrible receiver who fights the football even on simple routes. Will have to serve as the power portion of a committee or else be content with coming out on third down at the NFL level. Bigger backs like Foreman have gone bust often in the NFL though so he is far from a sure thing despite the glittering college numbers.

Wayne Gallman (Clemson) 6-0 215 4.52: Versatile runner who is adept both carrying and catching the football. Gallman finds the hole quickly and uses good burst to pick up yardage. Has developed nicely into a receiving back; showing good hands to pluck the football out of the air. Not a home run guy but Gallman has the pure speed to make big plays at a consistent level. Really struggled badly in pass protection which is not a small deal going into the NFL. Got run over more than a few times and playing time could be curtailed some if Gallman doesn't shore up that problem quick.

Samaje Perine (Oklahoma) 5-10 4.57: Your classic power back all the way. Perine is short on flash and picks up almost all of his yardage with a straight-ahead bulldozer style. There is little in the way of wiggle or shiftiness in Perine's game and he wasn't used much in the passing attack with the Sooners. Adept at keeping his feet moving and has the strength to break tackles moving forward. Junkyard dog runner all the way who is likely destined for the power role in a committee.

Corey Clement (Wisconsin) 5-10 227 4.53: Clement follows former Badger and current San Diego Chargers running back Melvin Gordon to the NFL. With good quickness and acceleration, Clement has drawn comparisons to Gordon. Another kid who knows where his blocking is and waits patiently for the play to develop. Can go from 0-60 in flash. True home run threat. Solid receiver but was not used much in that part of the offense while with the Badgers so the ceiling is unknown. Lacking in upper-body strength which results in a high number of plays where Clement goes down upon first contact. Won't be able to move the pile in short-yardage situations and had major injury issues in college, including a sports hernia surgery.

*Marlon Mack (South Florida) 5-11 205 4.54: Became the USC career rushing leader in 2017. Very productive player for South Florida over the last three seasons and consistency quite impressive as Mack has posted three straight 1,000-yard rushing seasons. While Mack is on the slight side, his impressive speed and burst allowed him to average 7.1 per carry as a junior. Even more intriguing is that Mack is a natural receiver out of the backfield who can help right away on that front. Again nothing too flashy here as Mack doesn't break tackles and goes down often upon first hit but his mid-round grade seems secure.

Brian Hill (Wyoming) 6-0 219 4.57: Beefy back who runs with good pad level and impressive power. Seems to relish running over defenders and can move the chains in short-yardage. Looks like strictly a runner as Hill doesn't impress on the receiving end and in fact was not used much there at Wyoming. Slated for the power side of a committee.

*Donnel Pumphrey (San Diego State) 5-8 180 4.43: The definition of a scat back, Donnel Pumphrey was a weekly highlight film for San Diego State during his collegiate career with his flashy running. Given the utter lack of strength and size, it will be interesting to see if Pumphrey gets moved to a slot receiver role in the NFL where he could make an impact. The speed is top-notch as Pumphrey can take it to the house almost every time he touches the football. Given the sudden breakout of the similarly-skilled Tyreek Hill with the Kansas City Chiefs last season, Pumphrey could be selected with that type of role in mind. Will clearly need to be on a snap count however.

*James Connor (Pittsburgh) 6-2 240 4.67: Just a great story here as Connor overcame what truly was a nightmare 2015 season that included a torn MCL and then a diagnosis of cancer. Having beat back cancer, Connor is a success story already just for getting back onto the football field last season. Now in terms of his game, Connor is a tremendous power runner who always falls forward and keeps the chains moving. Can take a hit and keep moving forward as his feet are always in motion. Has some snarl to him which coaches will love. Unfortunately Connor is quite limited overall in terms of athleticism as he lacks burst and quickness into the hole. At nearly 4.70 in the 40-yard dash, Connor's lack of speed is a big issue against quicker NFL defenders. May not be able to get much of a head of steam when taking the handoff at the next level which will further limited Connor. Faces a tall task making it in the NFL but everyone will be rooting for him.

Kareem Hunt (Toledo) 5-11 225 4.57: You want to see some more pure speed here but Kareem Hunt is one of the better receiving backs in the draft which will gain notice. Also despite the lack of burst, Hunt has good quickness and possesses tremendous vision that allowed him to pile up the rushing yardage for Toledo. Shows good juke moves and knee bend to make defenders miss and Hunt is a very willing blocker as well which goes nicely with his receiving prowess. Was a bit abused though while in college as Hunt received a crazy amount of carries during his tenure at Toledo. That could lessen his time as an NFL contributor due to all the pounding and Hunt has some collegiate injuries as well to bear this concern out. He also was suspended for two games in 2015 for an unknown team violation.

Matthew Dayes (N.C. State) 5-9 203 4.47: A shifty and quick back, Matthew Dayes' best attribute likely lies in his ability as a receiver. At just 5-9 and 200 pounds soaking wet, Dayes can't physically hold up to a high amount of NFL pounding which limits his running upside. When he does have the football, Dayes shows a nice initial burst upon taking the handoff and he waits patiently for his blocking to develop. Sometimes takes carries outside too often but Dayes can slip gaps as well with his speed. Willing pass blocker but Dayes gets pushed around noticeably on that front. Like the low pad level he runs with and that helps Dayes to push the pile a bit despite the lack of power. Upside player who could easily out-produce his draft spot.

Jamaal Williams (BYU) 6-1 220 4.57: Track guy who ran for BYU in that sport. Sat out all of 2015 to deal with personal issues but Williams came back with a very nice 2016 campaign for BYU where he ran with power and drive. Williams always keeps his feet moving and has the upper-body strength to shed tacklers. Fights for everything he gets on the field. Doesn't do much on the receiving side of things though, which keeps Williams as just a mid-round pick at best.

Aaron Jones (UTEP) 5-10 205: Durability is a concern here as Jones missed a slew of games while at UTEP and that calls into question whether or not he can hold up against NFL pounding. A slight 5-10 and 205-pound frame needs to be addressed in the weight room but Jones was a highly productive runner in college when on the field. Reminds you of Darren Sproles in that Jones is on the small side but he can break a play open either running with or catching the football. Has an explosive first step and acceleration that gets Jones into the clear quickly. While he can't block a lick, Jones has enough functional strength to ward off defenders with a stiff arm and fight for extra yardage. Could be a diamond in the rough.

*Devine Redding (Indiana) 5-10 208 4.54: Has rushed for over 1,000 yards in each of the last two seasons for the Hoosiers, while also collecting a total of 16 scores. Redding is a decent receiver out of the backfield and has solid overall size. Not overly flashy as a runner though and Redding lacks the top-end speed to be a breakaway threat. Picks up the blitz nicely and has a reputation for putting in the work.

Elijah McGuire (UL-Lafayette) 5-10 208 4.58: Has the look of a late-round pick given the fact McGuire is not all that impressive a runner due to a lack of speed but his receiving skills are a plus. Averaged a mediocre 4.9 per carry as a senior which won't turn heads but McGuire did go over 7.0 per tote as a sophomore and junior.

I'Tavlus Mathers (Middle Tennessee) 5-11 197: Played three seasons at Ole Miss where Mathers was a solid but unspectacular player before transferring to Middle Tennessee after sitting out a year in 2015. Mathers proceeded to go nuts this past season as he made plays all over the field both in the running and receiving game. Actually became the first player in NCAA history with 1,500 rushing yards, 60 receptions, and 15 rushing scores in one season which he accomplished in 2016. On the surface Mathers has tremendous numbers but Middle Tennessee is not a power conference school by any means. Mathers is also an older prospect at the age of 23. Again the level of competition was not great at all but Mathers' overall performance last season surely raised the interest meter around him for the middle rounds.

De'Veon Smith (Michigan) 5-11 228 4.59: Bit of a plodder who worked in a timeshare during his time at Michigan. Average per carry was never great (4.2 and 4.7 yards per tote the last two seasons) but Smith runs with good pad level and has decent thump to his game. Hands are decent but not otherworldly. There could be some untapped potential given the light college workload but Smith is nothing but a project.

Jahad Thomas (Temple) 5-10 188 4.51: Thomas is quite small for the NFL and he severely lacks in overall size to be more than a part-time player. Scored a ton of touchdowns while at Temple and was a weapon as a receiver out of the backfield. Likely destined to be a 7th-round pick or a free agent training camp invite.

De'Angelo Henderson (Coastal Carolina) 5-8 205: When you score a rushing touchdown in 32 straight games, you will get noticed no matter what school you play for. Obviously Henderson is a small school product who has a steep hill to climb to stick with an NFL team but his tremendous production at Coastal Carolina should at least net him a training camp invite. Level of competition makes projecting Henderson an almost impossible task but he shows good quickness and enough power to warrant attention.

LeShun Daniels Jr. (Iowa) 5-11 225: Built like a freight train, Daniels Jr. can run over or around you. Tremendous leg drive and a strong tendency to fall forward could net him a short-yardage role at the NFL level. There is a severe lack of pure speed though which won't allow Daniels to be much more than that if he does make it.

Marcus Cox (Appalachian State) 5-10 205: When it comes to small school kids like Cox, speed has to be part of the equation which he does possess. Had some impressive numbers during his collegiate career, which Cox achieved through a high motor and ability to slip tackles. Can block a bit as well which improves Cox's chances a bit.

Dare Ogunbowale (Wisconsin) 5-11 205: Former walk-on who literally ran with a chance to carve out playing time on the Badgers. Unflashy runner who gets what usually is given to him. Will catch the odd pass but Ogunbowale at best is a depth back at the NFL level.

Chris Carson (Oklahoma State) 6-1 215: Built solidly at 6-1 and 215, Carson can pick up some tough yards and keep the chains moving. Shows enough speed to bounce outside but Carson is mostly a straight-ahead plow guy who will need to be in a committee.

Tarik Cohen (North Carolina A@T) 5-6 180: Small school burner who could draw some attention based solely on the blazing speed. Would be a return weapon at the very least and a slot guy on third down as well if Cohen can find the right team. Extreme long-shot but Cohen does has possess the precious speed commodity.

***Elijah Hood (North Carolina) 5-11 220 4.59:** The junior from North Carolina is a power runner who will earn a bunch of points from NFL execs on the strength of his excellent ability to pick up the blitz. Fundamentally sound across the board as Hood makes the most of his good but not great athleticism. Improved greatly as a receiver as well. Mostly a straight-line runner who lacks wiggle and the ability to slip through tight gaps. Won't open up often when in the clear and Hood overall is more of a chain-moving back.

***Joseph Yearby (Miami Fla.) 5-9 207 4.52:** Sometimes you have to wonder whose giving these kids draft advice. While he led the ACC in rushing in 2016, the NFL profile on the Miami Hurricanes' Joseph Yearby is simply not popping. Yearby is not much of a receiver out of the backfield and he has not shown the speed to pick up yards down the field. At just 5-9, Yearby also is a liability in pass protection which is a huge negative in today's NFL.

Justin Davis (Southern Cal) 6-1 200 4.57: An ankle injury limited Davis in his senior season but he was not very impressive either way. Picked up just 564 yards and 2 scores in 2016 and Davis was not involved much in the passing game. Limited overall player who is very slow of foot for a back.

Joe Williams (Utah) 5-11 205: Had somewhat of a bizarre senior season as Williams abruptly retired from the team after two games but then returned later in the year. Williams is a tough and muscular power runner who is north-south all the way. Seems to run with snarl and an angry demeanor. Has very little in the way of wiggle or the ability to create space on his own. Could sneak in as a late round pick.

THE REST

Taquan Mizzell (Virginia) 5-10 194

T.J. Logan (North Carolina) 5-9 195

*Tarean Folston (Notre Dame) 5-9 215

*Stanley Williams (Kentucky) 5-9 196

Rushell Shell III (West Virginia) 5-10 220

Anthony Wales (Western Kentucky) 5-9 194

Khalfani Muhammad (California) 5-7 174

William Stanback (Virginia Union) 6-0 230

Barry J. Sanders (Oklahoma State) 5-9 198

James Flanders (Tulsa) 5-10 206

FULLBACK

Sam Rogers (Virginia Tech) 5-10 228

Freddie Stevenson (Florida State) 6-0 243

Anthony Firkser (Harvard) 6-2 220

Emmanuel Holder (Towson) 5-11 265

Nate Iese (UCLA) 6-2 250

Dakota Ball (Alabama) 6-2 262

WIDE RECEIVER

Position Grade: A

First Round Talent: Mike Williams, Corey Davis, John Ross, JuJu Smith-Schuster

Analysis: The wide receiver class is loaded as between 4-6 players could go in Round 1 and up to 10 among the first two rounds. This has also been a position that often has a lot of depth and a slew of late-round picks that have really panned out.

*Mike Williams (Clemson) 6-3 205 4.48: Just the latest in a recent explosion of talented wideouts coming out of the school, Clemson's Mike Williams should be the top receiver off the board during the early stages of the 2017 NFL Draft. Williams has come a very long way from the incredibly scary fractured neck he suffered when hitting the goal post against Wofford in the team's 2015 opener; a scene that included him laying motionless amid initial fears he could be paralyzed. Having made his way back for the 2016 opener, Williams became the number 1 weapon of QB DeShaun Watson on the way to catching 84 catches for 1,171 yards and 10 scores in the regular season. While Williams does suffer from the case of the dropsies from time-to-time, his physical makeup is how you would draw up a future star receiver. Combining terrific size and explosion off the snap, Williams gets where he wants to go on the field who was a big-play machine for the Tigers. Once the ball is snapped, Williams opens up space quickly on his defenders and uses his muscular frame to fight for the ball. What Williams can work on is his route running which is not always smooth. Tends to cut off routes early and again he drops some passes which might call into question his concentration. Otherwise Williams is set to be an 80-catch guy right away.

NFL Comparison: Demaryuis Thomas

*John Ross (Washington) 5-11 190 4.50: While Ross is on the smaller side at just under 6-feet tall, he has the makeup and athleticism to be a supreme slot receiver in the NFL in the mold of a Julian Edelman or Brandin Cooks. Was once clocked at a ridiculous 4.25 while at Washington in the 40 which speaks to Ross' explosiveness. Upon the snap, Ross gets into his routes in a flash and generates separation with just a few strides. Served time at cornerback and was a big return weapon for Washington during his collegiate career which speaks to Ross' versatility. Great balance for a smaller wideout and Ross will hit the end zone if he gets even a bit of daylight. Route running is just all right as Ross relies too much on his speed in freelancing a bit. MAJOR injury concern as Ross suffered a torn ACL and a separate torn meniscus at Washington. Needs to stay in the slot or he will be dealing with more injury problems at the NFL level.

NFL Comparison: Brandin Cooks

JuJu Smith-Schuster (Southern Cal) 6-2 220 4.52: Possession wideout who has to answer some speed questions prior to the draft. Was completely shut down against top Alabama cornerback prospect Minkah Fitzpatrick in last season's opener which was concerning. Smith-Schuster rallied though to put forth a very good season in catching 63 passes for 781 yards and 9 scores. Smith-Schuster grades out well above-average in the size and strength department and his physicality with the ball in his possession is very impressive. Fights for extra yardage once making the catch and Smith-Schuster also gets where he wants to go on his routes given a strength advantage against most DB's. Unfortunately Smith-Schuster doesn't have a lot of explosion and he struggles to open up space between himself and defensive foes. Receivers with Smith-Schuster's lack of speed have often gone bust in the NFL and USC has a very bad recent track record sending players from this position to the NFL as well (Mike Williams, Dwayne Jarrett). Major bust potential.

NFL Comparison: Laquan Treadwell

Corey Davis (Western Michigan) 6-3 213 4.52: Yes Western Michigan is a smaller school but 91 receptions for 1,427 yards and 18 touchdowns is extremely impressive no matter what level. Those were the numbers accumulated by Corey Davis in 2016 which sets him up as a first round pick. Davis is super-athletic, which is evident by his instant acceleration once the ball in his hands. While Davis is not exceptionally quick off the snap, his route running is as good as any wideout in the game. Can fight for the football with good upper-body strength as well. What is perhaps most exciting about Davis is the fact he already has a vast array of moves and stutter-steps that make him a nightmare to cover. While he does have good height, Davis' jumping ability is not as good as you would like to see and he often lost battles in tight around the red zone.

NFL Comparison: Emmanuel Sanders

Curtis Samuel (Ohio State) 5-11 200 4.44: Meet the next Percy Harvin as Ohio State's Samuel possesses almost the same exact athletic and offensive profile. Just like with Harvin, Samuel is an explosive runner and a very adept receiver as well. He could be used both at running back and wide receiver in the NFL like Harvin was or possibly convert to the latter position completely. Samuel's calling card is pure speed that makes him a home run threat almost any time he touches the football and he is well-built in terms of strength to help fight through tackle attempts. Samuel is a bit on the small side but he plays with good knee bend when running with the football and has excellent change-of-direction skills. With Harvin not developing into the player he was in college however, Samuel could draw some raised eyebrows when determining if he too could fall down the same path.

Dede Westbrook (Oklahoma) 5-11 175 4.44: Another extremely productive slot receiver in college, Westbrook comes off a dominant 2016 campaign with the Sooners where he hauled in 74 passes for 1,465 yards and a monster 16 touchdowns. Westbrook exploits mismatches in the slot as he gets off the snap in a flash and reaches top speed in just a few steps. Runs precise routes which constantly had him open on short-to-intermediate routes. Is a complete string-bean physically as Westbrook is just 175 pounds soaking wet. Has injury issues in his past and that figures to also be a problem against more physical NFL DB's. Limited overall in where he can play but Westbrook always seems to get his numbers.

*Ar'Darius Stewart (Alabama) 6-0 204 4.55: Picked up 8 touchdown catches on a modest total of 54 receptions. That was tremendous production when you consider that Stewart was hurt for large stretches of the season. Stewart possesses a terrific set of hands that hardly ever let the football hit the ground and he uses his long arms to expand his catch radius. Adept at finding the soft spot in the coverage but route running still a bit of a work in progress. Gets by a bit too much on pure athleticism and not so much with physicality. Good upside.

Amara Darboh (Michigan) 6-1 215 4.59: Darboh performed solidly for the Wolverines in his career there but he also didn't exactly light things up with the numbers. Possession wideout who plays with a physical edge as most Jim Harbaugh players do. Successfully fights off jams with good leg drive and upper-body strength to get where he wants to go. Darboh has good hands and can go up and get it. Very good blocker as well. Lacks flash and won't make many big plays down the field. Overall Darboh is a limited player but a solid one at his present level.

Cooper Kupp (Eastern Washington) 6-2 215 4.57: The level of competition was lacking but Cooper Kupp has earned notice given the Madden video game numbers going back to his freshman year at Eastern Washington. Caught 117 passes for 1,170 yards and 17 scores as a senior in 2016 which shows his level of dominance there. Kupp is very quick in and out of his cuts and you can't get a better set of hands. While Kupp has speed in short bursts, he will pretty much be a catch-and-done wideout since there is not much in the way of acceleration. Faces the standard learning curve in undertaking a massive step up in competition.

Isaiah Ford (Virginia Tech) 6-1 190 4.53: Speed, speed, and more speed. Explosion and big plays are the name of the game here as Ford took the top off of many collegiate DB's while with the Hokies. While the 40-time doesn't classify Ford as a pure burner, he gets off the snap very quickly and his smooth strides allow him to get up to top speed within seconds. Not overly physical; Ford gets pushed off a bit too many routes for my liking. Needs to add weight and get into the gym to fight against jams. Receivers who can't beat jams are always a bit risky in the draft but Ford was productive from the start in college. Also Ford needs to work on his hands as he catches with his body way too often.

Zay Jones (East Carolina) 6-1 197 4.53: Was seriously insane with his production in 2016 as Jones caught 158 passes for 1,746 yards and 8 touchdowns for East Carolina. In the process Jones broke the NCAA record for receptions in a season which was a mark held by former alum Justin Hardy. The fact Justin Hardy has been nothing but a depth wideout on the Atlanta Falcons since being drafted shows you how the offense at East Carolina tends to skew the true abilities of the team's receivers. Jones is physically on the small side and his skinny frame will likely give him problems against press coverage and man-to-man on the outside. Has to operate in the slot or he won't make it.

*Malachi Dupre (LSU) 6-2 190 4.55: Dupre's collegiate numbers deserve an asterisk given the fact the LSU Tigers operated a heavy run-based attack behind Leonard Fournette during his time as a starter. Also the simply brutal QB play the last two years for the Tigers further stunted Dupre's progress. Not overly quick or explosive, Dupre's strength lies in his physicality and nose for the end zone. Goes up and fights for the football and gets off press coverage nicely. His good vertical leap will also make Dupre a jump-ball candidate on the outside. Overall the kid has untapped potential which could start to show itself in the NFL.

*Noah Brown (Ohio State) 6-2 222 4.48: Former four-star recruit who didn't get onto the field consistently until 2016. Obviously lacks experience and Brown had his entire 2015 wiped out with a preseason knee injury. Solid athlete who shows good straight-line speed and the ability to adjust his route on the fly. Inconsistent route runner overall however and Brown also struggles to get himself into the play when jammed at the line of scrimmage. Has to get up to speed learning-wise but Brown has the athletic skill set to serve as a decent prospect.

*Travis Rudolph (Florida State) 6-1 189 4.56: Once Jameis Winston went to the NFL, Travis Rudolph's numbers suffered as the Seminoles passing attack as a whole struggled. While Rudolph's overall statistics were not flashy, he did the best with what he had as the team's possession wideout. Rudolph has decent route running ability but he doesn't have the speed or acceleration you would like to see. While not much of a play-maker, Rudolph is a classic overachiever who makes the most of his limited ability.

*Artavis Scott (Clemson) 5-11 190 4.52: Like when Sammy Watkins and Martavis Bryant were running mates at wide receiver, so was Artavis Scott and Mike Williams for the Tigers in 2016. Clearly overshadowed by Williams, Scott was no slouch himself as he caught 71 balls for 592 yards and 5 scores. Clutch kid who made some big plays when the stakes were the highest. Has caught as many as 93 passes in college and so Scott profiles as a decent slot receiver with some untapped potential.

*Chris Godwin (Penn State) 6-1 205 4.53: The speed stands out here as Godwin uses his athleticism to complement excellent route running ability. Was a very good red zone TD producer for the Nittany Lions as Godwin used his above-average jumping ability to make the tough catch. Needs to add weight to get by the jam from opposing defenders though and Godwin also seem hesitant to get his nose dirty.

*Carlos Henderson (Louisiana Tech) 5-11 191: Slot kid who has tremendous speed and explosion off the snap. Comes off an 82-catch season for Louisiana Tech, as Henderson showed a strong knack for finding the soft spot in the defense. Henderson also gets in and out of his cuts rapidly with little wasted movement. Was used as a running back at times in college and Henderson can also contribute as a returner. Clearly a finesse kid as Henderson gets easily pushed off his routes and he won't win many jump balls given the lack of height.

Ryan Switzer (North Carolina) 5-10 185 4.57: A good deal of the hype surrounding North Carolina QB Mitch Trubisky was due in part to the contributions of the team's ace wideout Ryan Switzer. Switzer made plays all over the field for the Tar Heels and played much bigger than his smallish size would indicate. Route running is as sharp as any other player at his position in the draft and Switzer has incredibly soft hands that make him a very dependable target. Also was an ace return man which adds to the potential value. Needs to be in the slot given the size and strength limitations as Switzer will be pushed off routes and eliminated from more than a few plays unless he adds some bulk. What holds Switzer back from being more than a mid-round pick is his lack of burst or acceleration. Switzer doesn't often open up daylight when the ball is in his hands and so he is not anything near a home run threat either.

*****Taywan Taylor (Western Kentucky) 6-0 195 4.52:** Earned an invite to the Senior Bowl off a 98-catch for 1,730 yards and 17 touchdowns campaign in 2016. Needs to show he can separate from higher-caliber defensive backs both physically and speed-wise. Straight line speed is impressive but Taylor takes time to get to optimal acceleration. That is an issue that could easily hold him back against press corners. Has a good set of hands and is a smart player who often finds the openings the defense presents.

*****K.D. Cannon (Baylor) 5-11 180 4.47:** Very quick and explosive wideout who can be a return guy as a rookie. Gets in and out of his cuts nicely without losing speed. Play-maker who can take it the distance once in the clear. Is a finesse player who is not built to sustain a high amount of NFL pounding. Will be a slot guy or nothing at the next level. Has to show he can make the tough catch over the middle or be content on serving as a dime-a-dozen slot wideout.

Stacy Coley (Miami Fla.) 6-1 193 4.44: Incredibly quick and agile receiver, Coley has some of the best pure speed in the draft. Dealt with the up-and-down play of QB Brad Kaaya which curbed Coley's numbers a bit but he was a big play waiting to happen. Explodes off the snap and can open up distance on a defender with the ball in his hands. Tall enough to play the outside but needs to add some weight and strength to adequately grapple with defenders to get open. Likely going to get picked lower then he should due to the lack of numbers relative to other players ranked above him but this will set Coley up to be a bargain.

*****Shelton Gibson (West Virginia) 5-11 195 4.48:** Gibson can really run and his explosive release off the snap is a big play waiting to happen. While his hands are not consistent, Gibson has speed to burn and can take it to the house whenever he gets space with the football in his grasp. Needs to be much more disciplined when it comes to route running however. Gibson cuts off his route early when faced with a jam and he also struggled badly when trying to fight himself free from in tight. Could be too much of an all-or-nothing speed player.

Kenny Golladay (Northern Illinois) 6-4 213: Was a junior transfer from North Dakota and an All-Mac selection in 2016 as Golladay posted one of the best offensive campaigns in school history. In addition to catching 87 passes for 1,156 yards and 9 scores, Golladay rushed for another 192 yards and 2 scores on 20 carries. Versatile kid who is a tremendous handful physically. Will easily out-jump defenders with his 6-4 size and this will be a huge weapon near the end zone. Not a polished route runner though and Golladay often relies too much on his size advantage to make plays. This won't work as well at the NFL level of course given the uptick in competition. Doesn't have impressive pure speed but it is functional at least. Love the offensive scheme at Northern Illinois which helps add to the mid-round appeal of Golladay.

Travin Dural (LSU) 6-2 203 4.49: Like with Malachi Dupre, Travin Dural was held back by the run-heavy approach of LSU and the team's shoddy QB play the last few seasons. Needs to make a good impression at the Senior Bowl given the lack of numbers in 2016 (just 28 catches for 280 yards and a single score). Really like the combination of size and speed here and at a more pass-heavy school, can easily envision Dural being a much more hyped prospect. Torn hamstring ruined his junior season so there are at least some injury concerns as well. Keep in mind Odell Beckham Jr. is a former Tiger who also dealt with the offensive road blocks at LSU and he instantly became a star as a rookie at the NFL level. Not saying Dural will make that quantum leap but he has the physical makeup and speed that often translates to success in the pro game. One of the best sleepers in the entire draft.

Trent Taylor (Louisiana Tech) 5-8 178 4.51: Caught 124 balls for 1,570 yards and 10 scores for Tech as a senior in 2016. Eye-popping numbers no doubt but again the level of competition needs to be taken into account. Very small kid physically which is a huge challenge for Taylor right off the bat. Incredibly short at 5-8 and a string bean at just 178 pounds which is trouble when trying to break free from NFL defenders. Slot guy all the way and Taylor could help his status by working as a return guy. Faces a tall task making it given the physical shortcomings,

Amba Etta-Tawo (Syracuse) 6-1 204 4.59: Like the smooth route running and advanced understanding of how to set up defenders. Gets off the line quickly but pure speed lacking. Possession wideout who will fight for the football. Can go up and get it around the red zone as well. Short on flash and big plays. Has to be content as a depth receiver as a pro.

Fred Ross (Mississippi State) 6-1 207 4.56: Despite Dak Prescott moving on to the NFL, Fred Ross was still a very productive wideout for Mississippi State last season as he caught 72 passes for 917 yards and 9 scores. Big and well-built, Ross is a physical handful for opposing DB's. Gets to where he wants to go on the field with a nice combination of route running and sheer will. Muscular kid who will win the one-on-one battles. Not much speed to talk about here though which keeps Ross in the possession receiver realm.

Josh Reynolds (Texas A@M) 6-3 193 4.55: Good luck trying to keep Reynolds from scoring touchdowns around the red zone given his immense height. Possesses very impressive leaping ability which expands on Reynolds' catch radius. Was never a big numbers guy given the speed issues but Reynolds can serve as a quality third or fourth wideout at the NFL level with his impressive height.

Billy Brown (Shepherd) 6-4 236 4.59: Very rarely do you see a wide receiver operating in a linebacker's body as the small-school Billy Brown does. A freak of a specimen given the 6-4 height and massive 236-pound frame that is packed with muscle. Of course the downside is that Brown is a plodder but he can immediately contribute as a red zone fourth wideout given the size. Has a ton of work to do coming from the poor quality of competition he faced but Brown's physical numbers almost guarantee a late round draft slot.

Darreus Rogers (Southern Cal) 6-1 215 4.57: Clear number 2 option behind JuJu Smith-Schuster in the USC receiving hierarchy. While Smith-Schuster was the big-play guy, Rogers settled for the possession role where his nice combination of size and strength played nicely. One of the better blocking wideouts in the draft and Rogers has decent hands that can make the tough catch. Struggles on the speed side of things however as there simply is not much in the way of burst. Rogers doesn't get much separation in his routes and he is unlikely to make much in the way of yards after the catch. Was virtually non-existent in the red zone.

*Chad Hansen (California) 6-1 195 4.54: Tall wideout who needs to build up to top speed. While it takes Hansen a bit of time to accelerate, he caught some deep throws while in college. Has the classic size and speed profile that a pro receiving prospect needs to possess. Is strictly an outside guy as Hansen doesn't change directions very well and his vertical is quite average.

Jamari Staples (Louisville) 6-3 195 4.58: Has tremendous height for a wideout which makes Staples a force in the red zone and also when going up for jump balls. Is a very lanky receiver physically however which will prevent Staples from winning a high amount of one-on-one battles. The hands grade out as above-average and Staples is very skilled at blocking. Not liking the route running at all however. Cuts off too many routes early and also loses track of the ball at times. Can't fight his way free when things get physical.

*Damore'ea Stringfellow (Ole Miss) 6-2 212 4.50: Should stay in school to gain some more seasoning as Stringfellow is a talented by flawed receiving prospect. Wasn't overly productive for the Rebels and hands were inconsistent. There are tools to work with though as Stringfellow has an impressive combination of size and speed. Built like what an NFL receiver should looks like so there is intrigue here. The bust of a rookie season that Laquan Treadwell had in the NFL in 2016 will give pause however since both guys have a similar build.

*Josh Malone (Tennessee) 6-2 200 4.50: The struggles of Josh Dobbs hurt Josh Malone and his numbers in 2016 but the kid still presents some nice late-round upside given the well built frame and speed he possesses. Showed a nose for the end zone and also the short-area burst to get open at a nice clip. Made a bunch of clutch catches while in college which is an often overlooked plus. Needs more seasoning on running routes and using his size to ward off defenders once he gets drafted.

Jehu Chesson (Michigan) 6-2 203 4.58: Tall and quick in short bursts, Jehu Chesson has skills that can translate to the next level. Very lanky though and averse to contact. Often gets dropped upon the first hit by a defender which limits Chesson's upside. Uses a nice stutter-step to set up defenders and then a decent burst to open up daylight. Locates the ball nicely but drops an issue. If some of the negatives can be smoothed out, Chesson has the athleticism to be a contributor.

Keevan Lucas (Tulsa) 5-9 195 4.52: Ultra-productive and big-play wideout for Tulsa. Big speed game that excelled against lesser competition. Combined terrific route running with an explosive first step to get himself constantly open. Lucas can also take it to the house if given enough daylight. Very short at just 5-9 which keeps him only as a slot man. Won't ever outmuscle a defender for the football and can't help you when in tight to the end zone. Sort of a gadget player who can make a name for himself as a returner early on.

*Isaiah McKenzie (Georgia) 5-8 170 4.42: Wow what speed. McKenzie can win a race against almost anyone at any position in the 2017 NFL Draft. As big a home run threat as you can get when McKenzie gets a hold of the football. Sketchy as a route runner as McKenzie relies way too much on his speed and not much else. Concentration issues apparent as there were a bunch of dropped passes for the Bulldogs. Will likely be drafted as a returner first and anything else he give you will be a bonus.

*Speedy Noll (Texas A@M) 5-11 200 4.36: Needs to stay in school. Relying almost exclusively on blazing speed as his path to the NFL. Raw and unseasoned player who needs to bulk up to supplement the speed. There is no denying that Noll is a tremendous athlete who has track star speed but he needs to figure out the finer points of the game such as route running and warding off defenders. One-trick pony right now but there is evident potential.

R.J. Shelton (Michigan State) 5-10 202 4.55: Underrated wideout for the Spartans who had a knack for clutch plays. Nothing jumps out about the physical makeup of Shelton but he is an overachiever who makes the most of his modest ability. Route running is pretty good but Shelton's hands are somewhat inconsistent. Possession wideout all the way.

Quincy Adeboyejo (Ole Miss) 6-3 195 4.48: Slight but tall wideout who never really took off numbers-wise with the Rebels. Appeared to be playing at half-speed at times and route running was shoddy. Could have done more with his size as well. Athletic enough to go up and get the football but needs to fine-tune the small stuff.

*Ishmael Zamora (Baylor) 6-3 220 4.62: Possession wideout who can pack a punch physically. Zamora relished blocking and making the tough catch while in college. Will be an immediate red zone threat given his 6-3 height. Extremely limited athletically as Zamora has only adequate straight-line speed and he can't create separation.

Gabe Marks (Washington State) 6-0 188 4.57: Was your typical big numbers product of the Mike Leach system at Washington State. Marks has good short-area quickness and burst that allowed him to draw a high amount of targets. Not a physical player by any means and will have his hands full against the press. String bean body type is a big negative as well.

James Quick (Louisville) 6-0 182 4.54: Slot wideout who sense the seams in the defense and takes advantage. Could have done more with his athleticism in college and Quick will need to lift weights quickly in order to add pounds to his spindly frame. Candidate for fourth receiver duty in terms of Quick's NFL prospects.

Corey Smith (Ohio State) 6-0 188 4.43: Gadget player who will have to catch on as a return guy or a special teams gunner given the inconsistent offensive production. Can go 0-60 in an instant but Smith is a limited player whose all-or-nothing receiving approach places him firmly into the late round realm.

Zach Pascal (Old Dominion) 6-2 214 4.54: Made a name himself at Old Dominion as a TD-heavy wideout who has very good hands and the speed to create separation. As always in situations like this, Pascal has to go right to work adapting to a much quicker pro game. Fundamentals are sound so the kid has a real chance to make it.

*Ricky Seals-Jones (Texas A@M) 6-5 240 4.59: Massive wideout who has incredibly rare height for the position. Missed a bunch of the 2015 season with injury. Overall Seals-Jones is a very strong and tough receiver but he lacks the speed to consistently get open. Likely will work as a fourth wideout who comes in around the red zone.

DeAngelo Yancey (Purdue) 6-1 205 4.54: Up there in Boilermakers history in terms of receiving production. In terms of ability, Quick is enough of an athlete who gets by with size and strength as opposed to technique. He also is a rough route runner who seems to lose track of the ball at times. What Yancey needs to do is to hone his concentration and approach toward fighting off defenders. His skills on special teams could be his means to getting into the pro game at the pro level.

THE REST

Mack Hollins (North Carolina) 6-3 210

Garry Brown (Cal) 6-0 200

Janarion Grant (Rutgers) 5-9 176

Gehrig Dieter (Alabama) 6-2 207

Greg Ward Jr. (Houston) 5-10 185

Rodney Adams (South Florida) 6-1 190

Kermit Whitfield (Florida State) 5-8 180

Bug Howard (North Carolina) 6-4 210

Zach Pascal (Old Dominion) 6-1 216

Karel Hamilton (Stamford) 6-1 199

TIGHT END

Position Grade: C

First Round Talent: O.J. Howard, David Njoku

Analysis: While tight end has taken on more prominence the last five years or so as more NFL teams looks for pass receivers there, this is a top-heavy group that drops off quickly.

O.J. Howard (Alabama) 6-6 251 4.64: Former five-star recruit who is set to be the latest ultra-athletic tight end to make an immediate impact at the NFL level in the receiving game. Draws comparisons to Jimmy Graham or Jordan Reed in terms of uncanny speed and athletic explosiveness. Route-running is very impressive for such a big guy and Howard has very soft hands that make him a natural pass-catcher. Can really go up and get the football and will be an immediate weapon in the red zone. Despite the imposing size, Howard grades out as just a mediocre blocker and he has some finesse to him in terms of avoiding contact when possible. Also for all his athletic ability, Howard's receiving numbers at Alabama were not overly impressive as Nick Saban spread the football around. Be that as it may, Howard stands a very good chance of being a Pro Bowl tight end right away.

NFL Comparison: Jordan Reed

*David Njoku (Miami Fla.) 6-4 245 4.70: Terrific receiving tight end who blends above-average speed for the position with the physical edge to fight for the football in traffic. Njoku is also a top-notch red zone threat as he caught 8 touchdowns in 2016 and he comes from what many call Tight End U as he looks to follow in the solid-to-very-good NFL careers of Greg Olsen, Kellen Winslow, and Jeremy Shockey. While his blocking can use some polishing, Njoku has the potential to be the best tight end in the 2016 class.

NFL Comparison: Martellus Bennett

*Bucky Hodges (Virginia Tech) 6-6 245 4.67: Has been a big receiving weapon for the Hokies from the start as Hodges recorded the most productive offensive numbers at the position in the school's history as a freshman. Since that time, Hodges has cemented his reputation as a poor-blocking but excellent receiving tight end. Blends smooth route running ability with a set of hands that almost never drop the football. Finds the seam in the zone and has the speed to continue moving down the field once the catch is made. Still has some untapped potential. Rising.

Evan Engram (Ole Miss) 6-3 227 4.60: Has arguably the best speed of any tight end in the 2017 draft. Engram proved himself a handful in the red zone last season as he hauled in 8 touchdowns and he proved to be an impact receiver for the Rebels throughout his college tenure. Engram's blocking is downright comical which means he will strictly be used as a receiving option but he also could be moved to wide receiver given his quickness off the snap and solid route running ability.

Jake Butt (Michigan) 6-6 248 4.71: Michigan tight end Jake Butt became the rallying cry for those who argue that college football players need to be insured during meaningless bowl games after the senior went down with a torn ACL in the Orange Bowl. Prior to the injury, Butt was considered one of the better tight ends in college football as he combined good speed and an ability to find the seam down the field. While Butt's blocking is just as shoddy as most of the other top tight ends in the draft, the fact he won't be ready for the start of the 2017 season will undoubtedly cause his stock to drop.

Jordan Leggett (Clemson) 6-5 258 4.73: Was a wide receiver in high school who has the athleticism to split out wide or work in the slot. Is a walking mismatch due to the fact Leggett has a nice burst off the snap and gets into his cuts quickly. Can make plays after the catch as well which adds to the upside but Leggett has had his work ethic publicly called into question at Clemson. When it comes to the work ethic, Leggett sometimes gave up on plays when he was not directly involved and also his production tended to wildly fluctuate each week. Also Leggett didn't seems to care much about the blocking side of things. Given those negatives, Leggett could be taken off a few draft boards.

Cole Hiktuni (Louisville) 6-5 248 4.67: Really came into his own as a senior as Hiktuni hauled in 8 touchdown passes and really developed into a terrific receiver overall. Very hard-working kid who made his way through Sacramento State and San Francisco Community College before getting into Louisville. While he is a decent overall prospect, Hiktuni doesn't excel in any one facet. Speed off the snap is solid but route running can be a bit choppy. Takes a few strides to get up to full speed and not often will Hiktuni be able to open up down the field once he makes the catch. Like with everything else, Hiktuni's blocking passes the grade without wowing anyone and there is the chance he may already be as good as he is going to get.

Gerald Everett (South Alabama) 6-3 240 4.68: Small school kid that is catching a lot of attention and rightfully so. Was a member of the UAB football program and then landed in South Alabama when the former discontinued football. What is really obvious here is that Everett has very impressive receiving skills that center on a knack of finding open seams and possessing a tremendous set of hands. Good luck finding tape of Everett dropping passes because it will be a long search. Some guys just have the "it" factor in terms of getting open and Everett possesses that knack. The blocking is horrendous though so Everett will need a lot of coaching there and ultimately will likely be just a pass receiving specialist in the NFL.

Blake Jarwin (Oklahoma State) 6-5 242 4.74: At this stage of the tight end rankings, you begin getting into the guys who are better blockers then receivers and Jarwin is that type of player. Caught just 19 passes in 2016 and was used mostly as a run blocker. There is a place in the NFL for Jarwin though as he takes good angles with his blocking and has the power to open up holes for the ball-carrier.

Michael Roberts (Toledo) 6-4 270 4.77: Massive blocker who combines way above-average power and a nasty disposition. Shows a nice base and knee bend when blocking in order to hold ground and his impressive leg drive can push defenders out of the play. While he is capable of catching the odd pass, that is not a big part of Roberts' game.

Hayden Plinke (UTEP) 6-4 255 4.72: Led all Conference USA in receiving touchdowns among tight ends with 8 in 2016. Smooth route runner and above-average receiver who plucks the football out of the air with a nice set of hands. Maintains his balance when hit and has the power to keep on chugging down the field. On the blocking side, Plinke tries hard but he grades out as just average there. Could be a decent sleeper pick in the middle rounds given the receiving skills.

*Adam Shaheen (Ashland) 6-5 227 4.87: Drawing a bunch of notice for being the rare D-II player who comes out of school early. Possesses tremendous size and a catch radius that makes Shaheen at the very least a big red zone target. Grades out as a top-notch receiver who runs crisp routes and has hands that hardly ever drop a pass. Obviously Shaheen has put up his monster numbers at the small-school level and adapting to the pro game is going to be a huge step up in class. Someone will give Shaheen a look in the middle rounds however as his receiving ability is eye-opening for a man his size.

Jeremy Sprinkle (Arkansas) 6-5 256 4.70: Receiving numbers with the Razorbacks won't wow you but Sprinkle has tools to work with there, such as possessing big height to serve as a force around the red zone and a decent enough set of hands. While he is a bit of a work in progress on that front, Sprinkle is a very good blocker who engulfs defenders with his wide reach to maintain position and leverage. Underutilized a bit with Arkansas, which means the kid has some decent untapped potential.

Eric Saubert (Drake) 6-4 242: Has to deal with the small school label but Saubert put up some huge receiving numbers at Drake last season that will gain notice. Saubert was second in the nation in average receiving yards per game among tight ends with 70.5 and he also was second in touchdown catches with 10. Clearly Saubert knows how to get open and work the seams of the field. Hands are arguably the best among all tight ends in the draft. Needs to get up to school on the much higher level of play he will face and chances of making such a leap are always a long shot when coming from a small school.

Scott Orndoff (Pittsburgh) 6-5 265 4.75: Did his part to boost the impressive Pittsburgh running game in 2016 with above-average blocking. Orndoff gets off the line quickly and drives forward with good power. Receiving skills are just all right as Orndoff fights the football a bit. Orndoff's route running is not very smooth either as he takes a few strides to get to full speed. A marginal prospect.

Josiah Price (Michigan State) 6-4 252 4.78: A bit on the light side for a guy known for blocking but Price overcomes that with terrific technique highlighted by an ability to fire off the snap at a rapid pace, while quickly getting into a defender. Plays to the whistle and was responsible for opening up more than a few holes for the Spartan runners. Price can also help in the receiving game as he hauled in 38 passes in 2016.

Darrell Daniels (Washington) 6-3 246: Constant injuries derailed what many thought would be a much more productive collegiate career as Daniels failed to become the big TD threat he was anticipated to develop into when first coming aboard to Washington. Receiving skills are shoddy as Daniels has stones for hands and he also has a terrible sense for finding openings in the defense. Run and pass blocking are solid however and that is where Daniels will have to try and catch on.

Pharaoh Brown (Oregon) 6-6 250 4.68: Another kid who failed to live up to expectations due to collegiate injuries. 2014 and 2016 in particular were a physical struggle and that makes grading Brown somewhat tough. A severe knee injury ended Brown's career at Oregon this past November and call into question whether he can stay healthy enough to grab hold of an NFL gig. Brown is a very good receiver who during his rare stints of health, showed a knack for getting open. The skills are there but Brown is going to have to settle for proving himself as a very late round pick.

George Kittle (Iowa) 6-4 250 4.77: Solid but unspectacular receiving tight end. Missed some games in college with various injuries, as Kittle is slight for the position and lacks strength. Tries hard on the blocking front but Kittle grades out as just average there. While he does need the football thrown directly at him, Kittle does have a nice set of hands and is somewhat adept at finding openings in the defense.

Jacob Hollister (Wyoming) 6-4 239 4.78: Should only be a late-round pick as Hollister doesn't do any one thing well but he was a solid performing at Wyoming overall. Hollister was one of the most productive receiving tight ends in the Mountain West as he combines good hands with a smart awareness while in his routes.

Cethan Carter (Nebraska) 6-3 240 4.71: Excelled in Mike Riley's system at Nebraska where Carter showed very good receiving skills and also graded out as a ferocious blocker. Rising up the board as Carter comes off solid seasons in 2015 and 2016 where he became a key part of the offense. What is obvious is that Carter is an athletic kid who can run good routes. While he needs to add weight, Carter carries nice upside.

THE REST

Anthony Auclair (Laval) 6-6 256

Jonuu Smith (Florida International) 6-3 245

Jason Croom (Tennessee) 6-4 246

Keith Towbridge (Louisville) 6-3 262

Derrick Griffin (Texas Southern) 6-6 238

Colin Jeter (LSU) 6-6 250

Daniel Montiel (Memphis) 6-3 240

Billy Freeman (San Jose State) 6-3 234

Mason Schreck (Buffalo) 6-4 250

Barrett Burns (Appalachian State) 6-4 250

OFFENSIVE TACKLE

Position Grade: B

First Round Talent: Cam Robinson, Ryan Ramczyk, Garett Bolles

Analysis: Offensive tackle arguably has had the most immense high-end talent the last few seasons but that is not the case for 2017 as there is a lack of franchise left tackles. Overall the depth is good but again not as impressive as recent years.

*Cam Robinson (Alabama) 6-6 326 5.20: The Alabama left tackle is set to be a top fifteen pick in the 2017 NFL Draft but he is not considered a Joe Thomas or Tony Boselli in terms of having the ability to develop into an instant 10-year Pro Bowl stalwart. There is no debating the tremendous power that Robinson brings to the table though and he has improved immensely during his Alabama career. Robinson shows nice knee bend and a quick reaction off the snap which helps him to instantly engulf defenders. A pure road-grading run blocker, Robinson opens up gigantic hole for his backs to slip through. His pass protection was very good in 2016 after some early struggles as a sophomore and junior but Robinson remains susceptible against pure speed edge rushers. The arm length is tremendous when sealing off the edge as well. Robinson's footwork can be a bit choppy however and this is especially true when moving laterally which is why he gives up some pressure against speedier ends. Not a pure can't miss left tackle by any means but Robinson should be knocking on the Pro Bowl door soon enough given his present ability.

NFL Comparison: Trent Williams

*Ryan Ramczyk (Wisconsin) 6-5 314 5.00: Yet another in a very long line of Wisconsin offensive lineman who turn into blue chip NFL prospects. Former D-III kid who really developed in the program. Waffled during his early college years in terms of commitment to the game and desire which Ramczyk needs to show is no longer an issue. Extremely athletic blocker who fires off the snap in a flash and can get to the second level with his well above-average speed. Shows excellent leg drive to hold his ground and move forward when run blocking. Technique is almost flawless both with his long arms and in the lower body. Has not had much experience against top competition as 2016 is the only season Ramczyk played at a D-I level. Unfortunately Ramczyk is a bit of an injury question mark as he needed hip surgery to repair a torn labrum.

NFL Comparison: David Bakhtiari

*Garett Bolles (Utah) 6-5 300 5.05: Thought Bolles should have stayed in school for another year given the fact he has just one season of starting experience at Utah after going the junior college route but Boles is trying to capitalize on a tackle class that is a bit less talented then in recent years. On skills alone, there is a lot to like here as Bolles grades out as an exceptional run blocker who combines very good speed and short-area quickness to stay in front of his man. Lacks a bit in the power department as Bolles is right around the 300 mark weight-wise. Can be bull rushed a bit but the biggest issue Bolles has is against speed rushers to the outside. While he has good speed himself, Bolles loses a bunch of it when having to shuffle laterally. Overall Bolles is rough around the edges as an unfinished blocking product but he could be a big-time player with further development.

*Roderrick Johnson (Florida) 6-6 308 5.15: This is another kid who needs more collegiate seasoning as Johnson was quite average in 2016 for the Seminoles. The big red flag here is that Johnson is quite lacking in strength and power which can be seen especially in the run game where he struggled to open holes. He also had trouble dealing with power rushers, often getting pushed back into the pocket. Johnson is a good athlete however and he does a nice job against speed rushers since he can move well laterally. Overall Johnson is in serious need of coaching at the next level and is likely to get drafted well above where his current skills suggest he should go.

Adam Bisnowaty (Pittsburgh) 6-5 300 5.28: Smart and experienced player who was a three-year starter at left tackle for Pitt. Tenacious and plays with a mean streak which coaches will take notice of. Gets the most of his limited athletic ability. Bisnowaty lacks upper-body strength which causes him trouble against bull-rushers and when trying to open holes in the run game. A right tackle prospect given the lack of athleticism and power.

Dion Dawkins (Temple) 6-5 300 5.10: This is a left tackle prospect that is rising quickly. There is a ton to like here as Dawkins has the athleticism and fluid movement in space to man left tackle in the NFL and his strength is functional as well. Has four years of experience as a tackle for Temple in a pro-style offense which counts as an added bonus. Broke his foot as a freshman but generally has been dependable when it comes to health. Has to work on keeping his feet constantly in motion and bending at the knees so he doesn't get pushed back into the pocket. Dawkins' strength is a big plus though and if he gets proper hand placement, can eliminate a defender from the play. High upside kid.

Antonio Garcia (Troy) 6-6 302 5.10: Could play left or right tackle in the NFL as Garcia has excellent blocking technique and has his head on a swivel when looking for defender to go up against off the snap. Garcia moves nicely both laterally and to the next level and his run blocking is very impressive. Has some issues while pass protecting against stronger defenders but Garcia always plays to the whistle. It is imperative for Garcia to keep good knee bend to try and remedy troubles again the stronger opponents but again the effort seems to always be there. Will go to the Senior Bowl where Garcia could boost his stock with a nice showing.

Taylor Moton (Western Michigan) 6-5 328 5.00: Moton has a good chance of being moved to guard at the next level given the fact his weight is more conducive to the inside. Very good pass protector who combined decent fluidity for his immense size. Slides laterally nicely and can get to the second level when run blocking. Was bull rushed at times due to an upward stance that needs to be corrected in order to maintain leverage.

Avery Gennesy (Texas A@M) 6-5 315 5.11: Coached by former Miami Dolphins O-line coach Jim Turner with the Aggies. Solid and well-built left tackle prospect who is catching a decent amount of late hype. Has played all over the line, including at center which speaks to the terrific fundamentals Gennesy has. Possesses good arm length for tackle and impressive agility for a guy his size. Runs into trouble with bull rushing defenders and work in the run game can get better. Impressive prospect.

Conor McDermott (UCLA) 6-8 310 5.28: Built like a basketball player with immense 6-8 height. Looks more like a right tackle candidate as McDermott grades out as a good but not dominant blocker in pass protection. Was more productive in the run blocking game as McDermott's size swallows up defenders whole. Like with most tall lineman, has to keep a low base or else he will get run over.

Chad Wheeler (Southern Cal) 6-6 310 5.20: Has as long an injury history as any prospect in the draft. Wheeler suffered a torn ACL back in 2014, has suffered two known concussions, and had a shoulder surgery in high school. Perhaps more concerning was a run-in with police in 2015 that got Wheeler suspended for USC's Holiday Bowl appearance that season. While Wheeler was not arrested, some will avoid him altogether given the uncertainty of his health both physically and mentally. On the field, Wheeler is a very good NFL prospect as he combines good burst off the snap and grades out above-average in pass protection. Having played in a pro-style attack, Wheeler was also terrific in the run blocking game. Has some pure power negatives but Wheeler would be graded out as a more much impressive prospect without the health/mental concerns.

Erik Magnuson (Michigan) 6-5 305 5.14: Did a nice job replacing Taylor Lewan at left tackle for the Wolverines. While Magnuson is not in the same class as Lewan, he more than held his own as a pass protector on the left side. Fires off the snap quickly and uses good hand-to-hand skills to keep defenders in check. Run blocking is only average and Magnuson does have trouble with power defensive lineman. Has been a guard for large stretches of his college career and could be an option there in the pro game.

Juli'en Davenport (Bucknell) 6-6 315 5.10: Love the size and combination of speed and strength which makes Davenport a very interesting small-school player. Has immense length and agility to man the left side in the pros. Davenport needs more than a little work on his technique to make it though as he relied way too much on his strength against lesser competition. Can be bull rushed due to mediocre upper-body strength as well. Needs seasoning for sure but Davenport is a clear upside pick.

Dan Skipper (Arkansas) 6-9 319 5.44: Can only be a right tackle prospect as Skipper is slow as molasses and struggles badly with speed rushers. Could even be moved inside if need be. What Skipper does do very well though is open large holes in the run game; firing off the snap with good technique to neutralize his defensive opponent. Shows toughness and plays with a nasty demeanor.

Will Holden (Vanderbilt) 6-7 313 5.18: Right tackle prospect who has good strength but not much in the way of athleticism. Works a bit too upright in pass protection which gets exposed against more agile defenders. Lateral quickness not a strength. Can be a very good run blocker at the next level which will be Holden's main contribution to the team that brings him aboard.

Levon Myers (Northern Illinois) 6-5 309 5.30: Good pass protector who helped combine with Max Scharping to give up the second-fewest sacks as a team in the country. Solidly built kid who gets off the snap quickly and uses good hand placement to maintain leverage. Tries hard in the run-blocking game but Myers much less effective there given a lack of fluidity and the speed to move forward in the play.

J.J. Dielman (Utah) 6-5 300 5.20: Was constantly hurt during his Utah career and before having his 2016 season cut short with an injured foot, Dielman was moved to center. The pluses here are that Dielman has experience all over the line but physically he doesn't seem to be able to withstand consistent pounding. At just 300 pounds, Dielman needs to gain weight and power to stay on the field. Decent player both in the pass protecting and run game but Dielman may need to be a backup lineman at least initially as he works on adding bulk.

Storm Norton (Toledo) 6-8 306 5.18: Toledo put up all sorts of offensive numbers in 2016 on the strength of their offensive blockers neutralizing the defensive lines they went up against. Norton is an accomplished pass blocker and decent enough run blocker against the weaker competition that Toledo faced but he is likely slated for backup duty in the NFL given the overall average skills.

Jonathan McLaughlin (Virginia Tech) 6-5 292 5.28: Very slight for an offensive lineman at under 300 pounds. Athletic and agile kid who can get out against speed rushers but struggled when dealing with bull rushing opponents. Has to work at right tackle given the strength limitations.

Nate Theaker (Wayne State) 6-5 305 5.10: Small-school kid gained a sixth year of eligibility after missing all of 2015 due to undergoing back surgery. Drawing attention due to a very interesting combination of size and agility. Will either have to play right tackle or move to the inside to guard at the pro level. It is tough to evaluate Theaker given the level of competition but his measureables are impressive and the fundamentals check out.

Joe Heck (North Carolina) 6-6 300 5.09: Was a right tackle for North Carolina but likely will be moved to the inside once drafted. Struggled when pass blocking as Heck doesn't move well laterally and was a bit slow off the snap. Has to play with better knee bend as well. Grades out above-average in the run blocking department, which gives more reasoning to placing Heck inside.

Michael Dunn (Maryland) 6-5 300 5.21: Injury-prone blocker who is just average across the board. Can maybe make it as a right tackle but likely needs to be backup for a few years while he works out technique issues.

Jemar Clark (Arkansas State) 6-5 306 5.09: Offensive linemen from small schools like Jemar Clark have a higher success rate of making it in the NF than at most other positions. Clark is fundamentally sound and smart and often takes the right angles in pass protection. Shows a very good setup and tries hard when it comes to run blocking.

Andreas Knappe (UCONN) 6-8 319 5.20: Could go in the seventh round or net a free agent invite. Tall and rangy, Knappe's long arms make him a decent pass blocker. Loses himself in space though as Knappe doesn't run well and struggles to consistency help in the run game.

Victor Salako (Oklahoma State) 6-5 335 5.45: Has to move inside as Salako's weight is more conducive to playing guard in the NFL and his utter lack of fluidity will get exposed on the outside. Works well in tight as Salako has very good strength but he is a purely stationary blocker.

Cole Croston (Iowa) 6-5 307 5.07: Well-built tackle who held up well in pass protection and did just enough to grade out as average opening holes in the run game. Croston has a wide base and long arms that help engulf defenders but he comes off the snap too slow which gets him into trouble against speed rushers. Borderline prospect.

Javarious Leamon (South Carolina State) 6-7 328 5.39: Big and powerful blocker who comes off the snap quickly to engage. Possesses good balance and hand-to-hand skills to keep defenders neutralized. Leamon does lack lateral quickness however and has a rough time getting himself back into position when he loses a step while blocking. Also remains susceptible to being pushed backwards given Leamon's habit of not properly bending his knees in tight.

THE REST

Justin Senior (Mississippi State) 6-5 322

Sam Tevi (Utah) 6-5 312

Jerry Ukowe (William & Mary) 6-7 318

Colin Buchanan (Miami Ohio) 6-5 319

Kent Perkins (Texas) 6-5 320

Mitchell Kirsch (James Madison) 6-5 300

Jonah Pirsig (Minnesota) 6-8 315

Max Rich (Harvard) 6-6 310

Daniel Brunskill (San Diego State) 6-5 278
Clint Van Horn (Marshall) 6-5 317

CENTER

Position Grade: D

First Round Talent: NONE

Analysis: Center annually is a weak position with just a handful of guys who even have a chance of becoming a starter. 2017 is no different as there is nary a first-round talent in the bunch.

Ethan Pocic (LSU) 6-7 309 5.39: Very tall for a center but Pocic was terrific in helping the LSU Tigers turn into one of the best running teams in the country last season. Athletic center who explodes off the snap and has the speed/athleticism to block into the second level. Shows good knee bend when blocking to keep leverage and to help deal with a lack of pure strength. Opens nice holes while operating in the run game but bull rushing defensive tackles are a bit of a struggle for Pocic. Easily the top center in the draft who could earn a second round pick.

Pat Elfein (Ohio State) 6-3 300 5.29: Dependable member of the top-notch Ohio State Buckeyes offensive line that helped put Ezekiel Elliott on the map. Elfein is a smart and steady center whose low base and technical approach turned him into a very good run blocker. Has good upper-body strength but Elfein struggled at times in pass protection and likely will need a move to center in the NFL. Played guard extensively for Ohio State so he has experience along the line.

Tyler Orlosky (West Virginia) 6-3 295 5.18: A bit of a finesse player who depends on leverage and agility to keep defenders at bay. Gets off the snap quickly and has the quickness to slide laterally to block. Tall but very light. Struggles one-on-one against bigger defensive lineman. Has to play center in the NFL as he is too light to be a guard.

Kyle Fuller (Baylor) 6-5 315 5.24: Has played both at guard and center for the Baylor. Can make it at either spot given his impressive size and strength combination. Held up well in pass protection and run blocking. Didn't excel in either but Fuller was an overall dependable lineman.

Jon Toth (Kentucky) 6-5 310 5.05: Seems more suited to play guard as Toth doesn't have much in the way of pure power and his inconsistent performances in college make manning the important center spot not a great match. Eager blocker who has nice agility and speed to help in the run blocking game. Gets to the second level nicely. Plays with good leverage and knee bend but often gets beat by quicker and more powerful defensive lineman while in pass coverage.

Cameron Tom (Southern Miss) 6-4 290 5.00: Solid and consistent blocker but Tom needs to get into the weight room to remedy a very slight frame. Needs help against stronger defenders given his poor upper-body strength. Keeps his head on a swivel constantly and plays with decent leverage and a low stance. Shows good awareness and technical skills but Tom has some work to do before he can be an NFL starter.

Jay Guillermo (Clemson) 6-3 310 5.32: Had an excellent junior season for the Tigers but Guillermo was noticeably less efficient in 2016. Strong and stout blocker who does a nice job while pass protecting but Guillermo gets in trouble with speedy players. Not a good run blocker by any means and Guillermo had issues opening up consistent holes for his runners.

Tobijah Hughley 6-2 295 5.15: Marginal center prospect as Hughley gets by too much on technique which will get exposed at a higher rate at the NFL level. Very light and tall for a center which is not an ideal combination either. Gets off the snap nicely and uses good laterally quickness to stay in front of his man. Can get to the second level while run blocking but gave up way too much pressure to pass rushers.

Lucas Crowley (North Carolina) 6-2 290 5.10: Could catch on as a backup center or guard as a late-round pick. Lauded for work ethic and junkyard dog approach. Overcomes lack of strength with good leverage while blocking. Seems more suited for guard as Crowley needed help often when at center in terms of pass protection.

Max Halpin (Western Kentucky) 6-2 295 5.09: Caught some attention at a small school as Halpin was a very good center both in the run blocking and pass blocking game. Needs to add some weight to battle NFL defenders but technique is generally solid. Has good hand placement off the snap and keeps his head moving to stay on top of opposing defensive players.

THE REST

Freddie Burden (Georgia Tech) 6-3 299

Cam Keizur (Portland State) 6-4 322

Jamaal Clayborn (Mississippi State) 6-3 316

Anthony McMeans (New Mexico State) 6-1 318

Alex Kelly (Colorado) 6-1 310

Deyshawn Bond (Cincinnati) 6-1 292

Brandon Kublanow (Georgia) 6-2 288

Brian Gala (Penn State) 6-3 295

Michael Coe (North Dakota) 6-2 300

Joe Scelfo (N.C. State) 6-0 294

OFFENSIVE GUARD

Position Grade: C

First Round Talent: Dan Feeney

Analysis: Not much happening here in terms of top-shelf talent but guard is where you find many failed tackles who are lunch pail players.

Dan Feeney (Indiana) 6-4 305 5.15: Should be a guard at the NFL level but has experience at right tackle. Missed a few games with a concussion in 2016 but was lauded as a tremendous run blocker who helped put Tevin Coleman on the map. Incredibly strong kid who opens up gaping holes on power alone. Relies too much on brute force, with Feeney not always keeping his feet moving and playing with fluidity. While decent in pass protection, Feeney can be beat with speed. Despite these negatives, Feeney is a first round talent.

NFL Comparison: Josh Sitton

Dorian Johnson (Pittsburgh) 6-5 300 5.23: Steady and durable run blocker. Opened up gaping holes for James Connor with way above-average power and force. Inconsistent in pass blocking as Johnson plays too upright and struggles with quicker defenders.

Forrest Lamp (Western Kentucky) 6-3 300 5.16: Western Kentucky was lauded for their tremendous offensive lines over the years and that has helped gain notice for the dependable and fundamentally sound Forrest Lamp. While a bit light for a guard, Lamp has good height and underrated power to help both in the run blocking and pass blocking game. Plays with good leverage and a stout base. High-achieving kid who will put in the work.

***David Sharpe (Florida) 6-5 357: 5.40:** The size is not a misprint. Sharpe is going to have to move to the inside at guard where his insanely huge frame works better. Also Sharpe is severely lacking in agility and speed to man the outside and go up against edge rushers. Strength is extremely potent and Larry Allen-esque and Sharpe is a pure road-grader as a run blocker. Opens up gaping holes as Sharpe's long arms easily push defenders out of the play. Pass protection was very inconsistent given Sharpe's slow setup off the snap and inability to move well laterally.

Zach Banner (Southern Cal) 6-8 360 5.22: Was a tackle for the Trojans where Banner earned All-PAC-12 conference first team in 2016. Will need to move to the inside where Banner's insane girth and combination of height and strength work best. Banner has a ton of weight to move around off the snap and speed rushers off the edge will be a constant issue at the NFL level if he doesn't move inside. Obviously Banner has a huge base and wingspan that makes getting around him a major chore. Believe it or not, Banner can pull a bit in short spurts but he needs to improve his hand placement so as not to become susceptible to swim moves.

Nico Siragusa (San Diego State) 6-4 330 5.55: Stationary run blocker who opened up gaping holes for Donnell Pumphrey. Struggles to beat a turtle in a race but Siragusa is a monster in the power department who can take on two defenders if need be. Clogs up a ton of space along the line and can completely eliminate defenders with his long arms and brute strength. Pass blocking is quite average. Tends to grab and reach off the snap which leaves Siragusa open to being beat by defenders who can split gaps with speed.

Issac Asiata (Utah) 6-3 323 5.30: Played some at center in 2016 due to injuries along the Utes' line. The added versatility could help Asiata's draft grade where he projects as a gifted run blocker and just a so-so pass protector. Relies way too much on his upper-body strength and Asiata doesn't play with adequate knee bend which allows defenders to shoot around him. What he does do well is get off the snap quickly and Asiata's impressive power can lock up defenders in a jiffy. Footwork is poor as Asiata doesn't move laterally well at all.

*Damien Mama (Southern Cal) 6-3 325 5.42: Has had some pronounced weight struggles at USC. At one time Mama ballooned to 400 pounds which is a big problem. Anyone with Mama's size tends to struggle in pass protection and that is the case here as he doesn't move well laterally. Brutally strong kid who is very competent in run blocking however and will be a back's best friend in that area. Was not even a full-time starter for USC given the inconsistency of his play and increasing weight.

Jordan Morgan (Kutztown) 6-3 320 5.20: Received an invitation to the Senior Bowl based on a very impressive small-school career. Drawing comparisons to Ali Marpet as a small-school kid who was eventually picked in the second round by the Tampa Bay Buc's in 2016. Fires off the snap quickly and relies on top-grade power to hold up well at the point of attack. Upside player who will be a popular mid-round target.

Danny Isidora (Miami Fla.) 6-4 310 5.34: Was part of a Miami offensive line that allowed a ton of sacks on QB Brad Kaaya but also helped the Hurricanes have one of the best running games in the country. Anchors well in the middle and holds up well at the point of attack with brute power. Isidora shows better mobility than you would think for a man his size and he was a very durable player while in college. The issue here is that Isidora is slow off the snap and he gave up a high amount of pressure to speedy defenders due to his struggles there. Lunges when he falls a step behind and overall Isidora is a very inconsistent performer in the pass blocking game.

Sean Harlow (Oregon State) 6-4 310 5.14: College tackle who will move to guard at the next level given the fact Harlow's foot speed is below average. Where he does excel is in pass blocking as Harlow possesses good power and very impressive arm length to lock up defenders. Run blocking is only average though which will need to be improved on for Harlow to make it as a guard.

Jessamen Dunker (Tennessee State) 6-4 305 5.18: Got invited to the Senior Bowl as Dunker has good size and strength for an offensive lineman. Moves out of his stance quickly and has the lateral quickness to shift side-to-side in holding blocks. Doesn't always generate the leverage he should be capable of given the size but Dunker has tools to coach up at the NFL level.

Kareem Are (Florida State) 6-6 334 5.19: Power blocker who was a major reason Dalvin Cook put up the numbers he did in 2016. Are was a terrific run blocker whose immense girth and power opened up gaping holes along the line. Has to be coached in terms of pass blocking technique as Are flails too much with his arms and doesn't use the best hand placement to fully engage his block. Missed time last season with concussion symptoms.

Ben Braden (Michigan) 6-5 335 5.29: Standout blocker who was a consistent force along the Wolverines line in 2016. Plays with a nasty disposition as per a Jim Harbaugh team and Braden's wide base plows through defenders to open up running lanes. Lacks athleticism and flexibility in his blocks when in tight. Can get bull rushed under such a scenario.

Greg Pyke (Georgia) 6-6 313 5.20: Lacking in the athleticism department will mean Greg Pyke will need to move to guard at the NFL level. Lauded for his abilities in the run blocking game but Pyke and the Bulldogs offensive line gave up a ton of pass rushing pressure last season. Got benched at one point in 2015 due to struggles there. Packs a punch off the snap though and uses good power to generate push.

Corey Levin (Chattanooga) 6-4 305 5.20: Three-time selection as an All-American at Chattanooga. Stalwart blocker for the team who was a starter for three seasons. Has worked both at tackle and guard and can play either spot in the NFL if need be. Has to get up to speed against higher caliber of competition but Levin is solidly built and has the short-area burst to be a contributor real soon.

Alex Kozan (Auburn) 6-3 310 5.15: Steady and dependable blocker for Auburn. Kozan was coached well as he has good technique and footwork for an offensive lineman. Gets into his stance quickly and gains leverage with good knee bend. His impressive blocking technique allows Kozan to overcome some strength shortcomings. Gets pushed back against bull rushers though and loses one-on-one battles when not using proper hand placement.

Kyle Kalis (Michigan) 6-4 305 5.33: While he could use some more weight, Kyle Kalis is a former five-star recruit who held up well both in run and pass blocking. Of course being a five-star recruit, Kalis didn't quite meet expectations in terms of being a blue-chip prospect, a status which he is not. Has to play guard due to the fact Kalis is built solely on strength and not speed. If he does add some weight, the kid could easily exceed his draft spot in terms of impact.

Jake Eldrenkamp (Washington) 6-5 297 5.08: Was part of a Washington offensive line that often underperformed and became leaky in pass protection; an issue that turned out to be the main problem in their playoff loss to Alabama. While it was certainly not all guard Jake Eldrenkamp's fault, the veteran barely graded out as a plus blocker across the board.

Zack Johnson (North Dakota State) 6-4 331 5.29: The size is enormous and that alone will get Zack Johnson a long look in the late rounds. Takes up a crazy amount of space along the interior of the line which clogs up more than a little room for opposing defenders. Dominated with pure power at the small school level but Johnson is going to need to show some technique and refinement to make it in the pros.

Fred Zerblis (Colorado State) 6-2 305 5.23: In the mix for being a late round pick due to the fact Zerblis is an agile blocker who can get to the second level. While he is short in height, Zerblis plays with good knee bend and hand placement.

Has to add some weight as Zerblis is quite lanky for a guard and he was pushed back into the pocket too often due to shortcomings there.

Chase Roullier (Wyoming) 6-4 319 5.22: Shows good balance and a nice blocking frame. Fires off the snap in a flash and can get to the second level with decent speed. Inconsistent in pass protection but Roullier is a dogged player who will be one to watch late in the draft.

Josh Boutte (LSU) 6-4 342 5.54: When NFL personnel men talk about stationary blockers, this is the guy they are imagining. The girth and pure power is astronomical when it comes to LSU's Josh Boutte but strength only goes so far. While Boutte is a mauler who can control his area of the line of scrimmage, he has no agility to speak of and there is no lateral movement either. That leaves Boutte very susceptible to being beaten through gaps on either side of him. Also he doesn't play with great leverage as Boutte can't bend at the knees very well given the crazy size.

THE REST

Erik Austell (Charleston Southern) 6-3 290

Tyler Catalina (Georgia) 6-4 324

Gavin Andrews (Oregon State) 6-5 339

Mario Yakoo (Boise State) 6-3 326

Kofi Amichia (South Florida) 6-3 296

Caleb Peterson (North Carolina) 6-5 300

Parker Collins (Appalachian State) 6-2 295

Adam Pankey (West Virginia) 6-4 313

Ryan Leahy (Cincinnati) 6-5 292

Evan Goodman (Arizona State) 6-3 310

KICKER

Zane Gonzalez (Arizona State) 6-0 190

Jake Elliott (Memphis) 5-9 165

Adam Griffith (Alabama) 5-10 191

PUNTER

Austin Rehkow (Idaho) 6-3 208

Cameron Johnston (Ohio State) 5-11 195

Justin Vogel (Miami Fla.) 6-4 210

LONG SNAPPER

Cole Mazza (Alabama) 6-2 235

DEFENSIVE END

Position Grade: A

First Round Talent: Myles Garrett, Jonathan Allen, Solomon Thomas, Derek Barnett, Taco Charlton, Charles Harris, Carl Lawson

Analysis: The most talented position in the draft hands down. The 2017 defensive end class has the top player in the draft in Myles Garrett, plus a guy in Jonathan Allen who some make that same claim for. Between 6-8 guys from here could go in Round 1 which speaks to the massive amount of skill from this group.

*Myles Garrett (Texas A@M) 6-4 268 4.60: The best player in the 2017 NFL Draft, Texas A@M's Myles Garrett should be the number 1 pick on talent alone. Garrett is a ferocious pass rusher who uses his blinding speed off the snap to get the edge, while also showing the power to get into the backfield with a bull rush. Garrett also has tremendous balance and the ability to shed blocks. Wound up batting down a high number of passes and forcing fumbles as well. The one knock you can place on Garrett is that he can make some improvements stopping the run but that is nitpicking at the highest level. There is almost no doubt that Garrett will be one of the best sack artists in the game from the jump.

NFL Comparison: Jadeveon Clowney

Jonathan Allen (Alabama) 6-3 294 4.76: While Myles Garrett is considered to be the top talent in the 2017 NFL Draft, it is not a unanimous line of thinking as there is a faction that is in the corner of Alabama ace defensive end/tackle Jonathan Allen. It is saying a whole lot when Allen is considered the most talented prospect coming out of the insanely rich and fertile Crimson Tide program; a designation that is without debate. Having excelled both at end and tackle, Allen has tremendous versatility that adds an extra dose of value to his name. As far as production is concerned, Allen dominated at the point of attack as he picked up 8.5 sacks last season and 11.5 tackles for loss. What really makes Allen a unique talent is how he put on a bunch of weight during his Alabama career but lost nothing in the way of speed and numbers. You just don't see 300-pound ends who can rush the passer the way Allen does or who get off the snap as quickly as he has shown in college. Holds his own when in close and sheds blocks with impressive power. Can do a bit better in the run game but that is about the only knock you can make here.

NFL Comparison: Khalil Mack

Solomon Thomas (Stanford) 6-3 273 4.80: High character kid who was lauded for dogged work ethic. Very good performer across the board as Thomas racked up 7 sacks and 13 tackles for loss. Not an explosive pass rusher in the Myles Garrett mold, since Thomas doesn't have as quick an initial step but he uses good strength and overall speed to get the edge. Can generate push with a bull rush if need be which helps expand Solomon's rushing game. Ultimately could work best in a 3-4 system.

NFL Comparison: Cliff Avril

*Derek Barnett (Tennessee) 6-3 265 4.75: Very experienced end who has been a starter since he was a freshman. Barnett looks like he could compete in weight lifting competitions as he is chiseled and sports a very powerful frame. Anticipates the snap well, which makes up for lacking an explosive burst. Was able to rush the passer by either getting around the tackle or using terrific hand skills to fight his way up the field while in tight. Tends to get cut blocked however and Barnett did very little in terms of batting down passes. Overruns plays on occasion which call into question Barnett's pure instincts. There are some who feel he is more of an athlete than a player like a Mike Mamula and that is certainly a comparison you don't want as an end prospect.

NFL Comparison: Cameron Wake

Taco Charlton (Michigan) 6-5 272 4.84: Was a late blooming player as Charlton didn't become a firm starter until 2016 as a senior. Has experience as a tackle but did his best work on the outside where Charlton racked up 8.5 sacks in 2016. While he has only moderate strength, Charlton has great snap anticipation and the hand skills to fight his way free from blockers. Gives off the feeling there is more of a ceiling to tap into. Upside pass rusher who can work on the outside both in a 4-3 or a 3-4. Inconsistent run defender but got better as last season wore on.

NFL Comparison: Everson Griffin

*Carl Lawson (Auburn) 6-2 253 4.63: Lawson is a pass rushing monster whose collegiate career was undermined by injuries. The most serious was Lawson missing a huge chunk of 2015 after coming down with a hip injury that required surgery and having his 2014 completely taken away due to tearing an ACL. He came back with a big 2016 however as Lawson picked up 9 sacks in creating constant havoc in opposing team's backfields and in the process, reinvigorating his draft status. Strictly a pass rushing specialist as Lawson lacks the instincts and hand combat skills to be a high-end run stopper. Outside of Myles Garrett, Lawson may have the most explosive first step among all defensive ends in the draft.

NFL Comparison: Jason Pierre-Paul

*Charles Harris (Missouri) 6-3 255 4.77: Could work as either an end in a 4-3 or an outside linebacker in a 3-4 setup. Very quick edge pass rusher who racked up 9 sacks in 2016. Love the handiwork as Harris knocked down 2 passes and forced 2 fumbles as well. Gets off the snap quickly and has a good array of moves and counter-moves to get into the opposing team's backfield. A slight frame makes Harris somewhat of a liability in run prevention however and as a whole leaves him as a pass rushing specialist.

DeMarcus Walker (Florida State) 6-2 273 4.83: Perhaps no defender had a better start to the 2016 season then Seminoles pass rusher DeMarcus Walker who picked up a silly 4.5 sacks in the team's opener against Ole Miss. The big start was just the beginning point on a phenomenal senior campaign where Walker racked up an insane 15 sacks and 17.5 tackles for loss as arguably the most productive pass rusher in the nation. While the numbers speak for themselves, Walker is a bit stuck between being a defensive end in a 4-3 or an outside linebacker in a 3-4 given his uneven physique. Seems a bit too pre-occupied as a rusher; with Walker's run prevention game lacking. Tends to stop playing when initial rush is neutralized and his overall rushing game may not translate well to the pro game.

Jordan Willis (Kansas State) 6-4 250 4.75: Falling down the draft board a bit due to the rash of talented underclassmen who declared for the draft. A potential steal in that scenario as Willis has very long arms that constantly disrupt both passing and running games. Underrated pass rusher who doesn't get the credit he deserves as Willis picked up 21 sacks the last two seasons combined. Smart and fundamentally sound player who fights through blocks and has a non-stop motor. Coaches love this type of player and overall Harris gets most of his sacks through sheer will since he lacks the explosion that many of the top rushers have.

Tanoh Kpassagnon (Villanova) 6-6 285 4.72: Kid who fell through the cracks but now has quite a few fans among NFL executives given Kpassagnon's physical skills. Gets up the field in a flash as Kpassagnon has a tremendous first step. Chops off opposing blocks in setting himself free to get into the backfield. A bit tall for a defensive end and Kpassagnon gets himself in trouble by playing too high; an issue that gets him neutralized by anchoring lineman. Works best in a 3-4 system where Kpassagnon can react off the snap in a stance.

Tarell Basham (Ohio) 6-4 262 4.70: Picked up 10 sacks and 14.5 tackles for loss as a senior in 2016. Former defensive tackle whose stock really took off once put out on the edge where his speed plays best. Can gain the edge quickly with a rapid first step and good counter moves. Strictly a speed rusher as Basham lacks upper-body strength and the consistent ability to break free once in an offensive lineman's grasp. Has a non-stop motor and can even play back in pass coverage a bit if needed. Improved against the run as last season went along. Needs to add 10-15 pounds when stepping up the level of competition in the NFL.

Daeshon Hall (Texas A@M) 6-5 270 4.88: Yes the "other guy" on the opposite side of consensus number 1 prospect Myles Garrett. Almost the polar opposite of Garrett as Hall is an excellent run defender who only flashes occasionally on the pass rushing side of things. Slow of foot both off the snap and in space but fights free with impressive power. Limited prospect who some will say had inflated numbers due to Garrett being on the other side.

Hunter Dimick (Utah) 6-3 272 4.99: While Dimick is quite lacking in speed and burst, he makes up for it with tremendous power and a motor that doesn't stop. He did pick up 14.5 sacks using this mode of attack but the level of competition was a step down from a BCS league. Battled injuries while in college and ultimately could be shifted inside in a 4-3. Dimick could be drafted a bit higher then he should go given last season's sack total against lesser offensive lines.

Josh Carraway (TCU) 6-2 250 4.70: Small but very speedy end or outside linebacker. Disruptive pass rusher who can get out of his stance and up the field in rapid succession. Purely a pass rushing specialist as Carraway' run stopping game leaves a lot of be desired. Struggles to get separation in tight given a lack of strength and drive. Overpowered at the point of attack often and Carraway has to work in a 3-4 given his current makeup and skills.

Keionta Davis (Chattanooga) 6-3 270 4.90: Massive pass rushing force on the small school level. Racked up a ton of sacks and showed tremendous hand skills in knocking down a boatload of passes and forcing fumbles. Seems to have a nose for the football which can't be taught but needs a good showing at the Senior Bowl to hold onto growing stock.

*Garrett Sickles (Penn State) 6-4 250: Not liking the decision to come out early (at least as of this writing) as Sickles is extremely lacking in power and is a string bean physically. Has to rely almost solely on speed to apply pressure which Sickles does a decent job of but he also gets completely pushed out of plays given the size issues. The height enables Sickles to get his hands on the football via the batted pass and he also wraps up nicely when making the tackle given his long arms. Needs to find some buffet tables and fast to add some weight.

Dawwuane Smoot (Illinois) 6-3 255 4.72: Has some Olivier Vernon in him as a guy who generates heat but doesn't register a high amount of sacks. Possesses a very quick first step and good hand-to-hand skills to keep blockers off of him. Bit of a lunger when in run support and doesn't anchor well when in tight. Lack of bulk gets exposed in such a situation. Can chase down runners with impressive speed though and Smoot has a vast array of pass rushing moves to work with.

Bryan Cox (Florida) 6-3 269 4.77: Yes he is the son of the former NFL linebacker. Suffered a thumb injury that put a topper on what was a very poor and disappointing senior season. Was constantly injured in college which calls into question how much work Cox put in physically. Had zero sacks last season before suffering the thumb injury which added to the disappointment. Does possess good speed and strength like his father but the numbers tell a different story.

Derek Rivers (Youngstown State) 6-4 250 4.79: Career leader at Youngstown State in sacks. Unrelenting pass rusher who constantly caused chaos in opposing teams' backfields. Fights his way up the field with a combination of speed and hand skills. Has to deal with the vast uptick in competition in the NFL which is always the big unknown and will keep Rivers as a late round pick.

Joe Mathis (Washington) 6-2 255: Could be a true diamond in the rough as Mathis is not being talked about as much as he should. Mathis is a strong kid who combines his power and speed to generate pressure. Now he is not a burner by any means off the edge but Mathis get up the field through sheer will and determination that is never-ending. Uses the swim move nicely and gains good leverage with solid core power. What Mathis does not do so well is get the edge with pure speed and he lacks overall flash. Has very little experience as a starter however and will get knocked for that.

Deatrich Wise Jr. (Arkansas) 6-5 271 4.82: Situational pass rusher who had a poor senior season. Actually improved his previously shaky run defense while at the same time seeing his pass rushing game go the other way. Doesn't have the speed off the edge to consistently generate heat but the size is impressive. Rough around the edges.

Darius English (South Carolina) 6-5 245 4.63: Speedy but undersized pass rushing end or outside linebacker. Fits best in a 3-4 as English's utter lack of bulk could make him a big liability off the snap while playing end. What stands out is English's terrific first step and quickness off the snap. Can get the edge quickly and this approach helped him rack up 9 sacks as a senior. Doesn't do much in the running game given the size shortcomings and English missed a bunch of games in college as he struggled to hold up against the pounding he took.

Issac Rochell (Notre Dame) 603 290 4.80: Marginal pass rusher who on the flip side is one of the best run-stopping ends in the draft. Diagnoses plays quickly off the snap and gets into proper positioning to make the play. Could move to the inside where Rochell's run-stopping skills could be used more effectively. Lacks the motor and pure speed to contribute much when rushing the passer.

Keion Adams (Western Michigan) 6-2 245 4.79: Has flashed some very good pass rushing skills and graded out above-average in stopping the run as well. Highly productive kid on the small school level who combines decent burst with a good counter moves to break free of blocks. Effectively uses a swim move and dunks under taller blockers which boosts Adams' pass rushing arsenal. Weight is very slight however and Adams will get walled off completely on more than a few plays given his shortcomings there. Project well worth checking out.

Noble Nwachukwu (West Virginia) 6-2 275 4.83: Big-bodied end who does a nice job stopping the run. Plugs lanes with good power and long arms. Any pass rush Nwachukwu puts forth comes strictly from getting up the field with leg drive and strength.

Trey Hendrickson (Florida Atlantic) 6-4 270 4.80: While limited athletically, Hendrickson was constantly creating havoc in rushing the passer on determination and brute strength. Sheds blockers seemingly at ease with long arms and a tremendous first punch off the snap. Wraps up the runner nicely with textbooks tackling as well. Won't generate nearly the heat in the pros as he did in college, as Hendrickson won't be able to get by just on power.

Ifeadi Odenigbo (Northwestern) 6-3 250 4.82: Could snag a seventh-round spot but not likely anything more as Odenigbo is a limited player both physically and athletically. Needs to add a bunch of weight to hold up at the point of attack and knee bend not ideal. Tough kid who gets whatever he can on effort. Good tackle who can help stopping the run.

Lewis Neal (LSU) 6-1 264 4.65: Very impressive speed here as Neal has a very good first step and straight-line speed. Should be in a 3-4 on the outside as Neal's lack of physicality and height will neutralize him often at defensive end. Can get the edge given the speed but Neal was not a very productive pass rusher in college when it came to sacking the QB.

Terrence Waugh (Kent State) 6-1 262 4.81: Effective stopping the run but not much in the way of rushing the passer since Waugh doesn't have the pure speed to consistently help there. Lacks height but Waugh gets push using good leverage and knee bend in tight. Likely a free agent invite.

Avery Moss (Youngstown State) 6-3 262 4.86: Moss is quite slow of foot which will keep him as nothing more than a possible seventh-round pick. While he is stout at the point of attack, Moss can only generate heat when powering his way through blocks. The fact that he comes from a small school adds to the long-shot odds of him making a roster.

THE REST

Ken Ekanem (Virginia Tech) 6-3 255

Evan Schwan (Penn State) 6-5 253

Pat O'Connor (Eastern Michigan) 6-4 275

Fadol Brown (Ole Miss) 6-4 273

Karter Schult (Northern Iowa) 6-3 263

A.J. Jefferson (Mississippi State) 6-3 277

Cameron Malveaux (Houston) 6-5 277

J.T. Jones (Miami Ohio) 6-1 263

Alex Barrett (San Diego State) 6-2 255

*Al-Quadin Muhammad (Miami Fla.) 6-3 250

DEFENSIVE TACKLE

Position Grade: B+

First Round Talent: Malik McDowell, Caleb Brantley, Carlos Watkins

Analysis: Still a nice batch of talent here but a shade or two below recent classes.

*Malik McDowell (Michigan State) 6-5 276 5.35: While he dealt with an ankle injury that limited his play a bit in 2016, McDowell once again showed that he is arguably the best defensive tackle in the 2017 NFL Draft. Shows a very rare ability to bull rush an opposing lineman but also has the speed to slip gaps if need be. Plays to the whistle and has a never-ending motor that helps McDowell get the most out of his ability. Comes off the snap a bit too upright which can be coached out of him but it did leave McDowell open to cut blocks. Overall McDowell is a complete defensive tackle who should go as a top ten pick.

NFL Comparison: Kyle Williams

Caleb Brantley (Florida) 6-2 314 4.98: First round talent who collapses the pocket and is a constant disrupter at the point of attack. Gets off the snap very quickly for a man his size and extremely active hands allow Brantley to shed blockers or engage two at a time to free up the linebackers behind him. Short-area speed quite good and this allows Brantley to serve as an excellent run stopper. While he won't collect much in the way of sacks, Brantley taking up blocks will really boost those behind him. While Brantley's consistency was lacking at times, the effort was always there.

NFL Comparison: Jurell Casey

Carlos Watkins (Clemson) 6-3 300 5.15: The athletic and powerful Carlos Watkins is a supreme and rare pass rushing defensive tackle. While nose or defensive tackles are more known for collapsing the pocket and tying up defenders to free up others to get sacks, Watkins handles that aspect on his own as he picked up 8.5 QB takedowns last season for the championship-winning Tigers. He possesses very impressive straight-line speed and the ability to shed blocks with terrific hand skills. Watkins also drives forward with excellent power drive from the legs. For all his obvious skills, Watkins is not completely refined yet as he plays a bit too high and gets cut down by blockers on occasion. While he picked up a high number of sacks for a D-tackle, Watkins doesn't possess a big variety of moves to fall back on if his first move is stunted. More or else a power rusher only.

Chris Wormley (Michigan) 6-5 303 5.15: Could work as an end in a 3-4 but Wormley is also an accomplished defensive tackle prospect. Wormley has improved as a pass rusher throughout his Michigan career; combining long arms and good power to fight his way through blocks. More or less an "effort/motor" guy as Wormley makes plays through a strength game and not so much with agility. Grades out very highly stopping the run as Wormley uses his long reach to grab hold of the ball carrier and also to tie up the middle. Pass rushing moves are quite ordinary and straight-forward and Wormley is in need of diversity on that front.

Vincent Taylor (Oklahoma State) 6-2 310 5.09: Solid prospect who combines decent athleticism and size and there is some ceiling left to Taylor's name as he was a late-bloomer at Oklahoma State. As far as the strengths are concerned, Taylor picked up a decent amount of sacks through a power rushing approach. Can slip the odd gap but Taylor gets up the field mostly through his strength advantage and long arms. Quickly ties up blockers to serve as an impact defender in stopping the run. Won't wow you athletically and as a pass rusher but Taylor is a starting-caliber NFL player.

Elijah Qualls (Washington) 6-1 321 5.42: Your classic nose tackle as Qualls uses his massive frame to swallow up space along the line and clog up running lanes. Can take on two defenders at once through his very long reach and excellent strength. Anchors into the ground nicely and plays with leverage to collapse the pocket. Will pick up the odd sack but Qualls is a firm lane clogging tackle.

*Davon Godchaux (LSU) 6-4 293 5.45: Very interesting but undersized tackle prospect who is capable of splitting gaps and who gets off the snap quickly despite the overall slow 40-time. Quite a disruptive rusher who can close on runners and make the play. Comes off the snap too upright however and Godchaux struggles in the run game due to lack of size. Easily swallowed up by defenders unless able to get through gaps off the snap.

Jaleel Johnson 6-3 310 5.10: Like the combination of size and athleticism. Johnson has proven he can get up the field both through speed and power which boost a defenders' stock. While not the most consistent defensive tackle in the draft, Johnson grades out as a slightly above-average pass rusher and a much more impressive run defender.

Dalvin Tomlinson (Alabama) 6-2 305 5.14: Terrific defender in the running game and Tomlinson has some of the best hand skills in the draft in terms of knocking down passes. Clogs the lane and takes on double-teams while anchoring. Lack of explosion or speed keeps Tomlinson mostly a run game defender but he more than did his part in helping Alabama gain the unofficial title of best defense in the nation last season.

Jarron Jones (Notre Dame) 6-5 315 5.34: Lots of injuries in Jones' Notre Dame career. Jones did finish strong however during his very good 2016 campaign in establishing himself as a run-stuffing tackle. There are some injury issues as Jones missed two games in 2014 with a foot injury and then all of 2015 with a torn ACL. Last season Jones showed the ability to collapse the pocket and get free into the backfield with brute force. Exceptional bull rusher who is impossible to move off his spot when he remembers to stay low but Jones doesn't always play with good knee bend as most tall players are inclined to do. Gets his hand on the football through forced fumbles and batted down passes but the drawback is Jones doesn't really generate much heat on the passer.

Montravius Adams (Auburn) 6-3 309 5.15: Impressive prospect on the physical standpoint as Adams has excellent size, speed, and strength. However he has been cited for lack of conditioning and a motor that doesn't always fire consistently. Classic case of a guy who has the tools but who doesn't always put them to work which will knock Adams 'draft grade down a bit. Picked up 4.5 sacks last season but with Adams' very quick first step and speed in short bursts, he should have had more. Could overachieve if he puts the work in or underachieve if the opposite takes place.

*Nazair Jones (North Carolina) 6-5 295 5.07: Probably could have used another year in school but this Tar Heel defensive tackle has very attractive speed and height for the position. If Jones can fill out some more by adding 20-30 pounds, he could turn out to be a steal in the middle rounds. Ran hot and cold during his college career; alternating good and poor games seemingly by the week. That could be a coaching issue or an effort issue which his NFL team will have to discover.

Larry Ogunjobi (Charlotte) 6-2 294 5.17: Someone will bite in the middle rounds on the athletic but light Ogunjobi. Rushed the passer pretty well due to possessing good short-area speed and a quick reaction off the snap and Ogunjobi can also split the gap as well. Run defense graded out as average and that figures to be an issue at the NFL level. Needs to bulk up quickly.

Ryan Glasgow (Michigan) 6-3 299 5.15: Consistently was able to tie up two defenders and also shed one-on-one blocks to generate heat on the passer. Stout in his stance and gets his long arms on a high amount of runners. Injuries derailed Glasgow's progress some. Much better run defender then pass rusher but that goes for most defensive tackles. Love the lunch pail attitude and approach and overall Glasgow could make for a terrific mid-round value.

Tanzel Smart (Tulane) 6-0 304 5.22: Earned an invite to the senior bowl after collecting 5.5 sacks and 18.5 tackles for a loss in 2016 for Tulane. While he played at a small school, Smart consistently got after the quarterback and interrupted the running game at a high rate. May not be more than a backup or rotational tackle in the pros but Smart could pay off after some development time is accrued.

Eddie Vanderdoes (UCLA) 6-2 305 5.11: Missed all of 2015 after tearing up his knee but came back in 2016 as a junior where Vanderdoes became a very impressive run defender. Can handle the nose tackle spot or work in a 4-3 in the middle. Engulfs blockers with good strength and drive. Almost a complete non-factor in rushing the passer however. Vanderdoes does bat down a decent amount of passes but will strictly be a run-stopper in the NFL.

DeAngelo Brown (Louisville) 6-0 310 5.20: Very powerful nose tackle who anchors nicely against the run. Stout at the point of attack and very tough to move off of his spot. Actively takes on double teams so those behind him can come up and make the play. Unselfish player who is a natural leader. Don't look for many sacks but Brown can make it as a starter somewhere.

*Charles Walker (Oklahoma) 6-2 304 5.14: Only was able to play four games last season due to concussion problems. Strong and quick interior lineman who can get to the quarterback at a high rate. Can slip gaps with underrated speed and agility but Walker struggles in tight since he is on the small side for a tackle. The lack of size will also not allow Walker to engulf two defenders to free up the linebackers behind him.

Jeremiah Ledbetter (Arkansas) 6-3 280 4.91: The speed really stands out here as Ledbetter explodes off the snap and can get into the backfield very quickly. Uncanny athleticism for a defensive tackle but the flip side is that Ledbetter struggles to escape a blocker's grasp in tight. Could be forced to move outside in a pass rushing only role given the very slight frame and Ledbetter also doesn't help much in run support.

Collin Bevens (Northwest Missouri State) 6-5 286 5.06: All-time school leader in sacks with 33. On the small school level, Bevens was a pass rushing fiend as he has a rapid first step and closes ground very quickly when an opening presents itself. Got where he wanted to go given the light competition but Bevens is a clear project that will likely need two seasons of schooling.

Josh Tupou (Colorado) 6-2 325 5.29: Monster of a man who eats up a whole lot of space. Clear run-stuffing tackle who can collapse the pocket with an impressive and powerful bull rush. Gets his hands into the passing lane and bats down a high number of throws. Statistics didn't leap off the page though and Tupou was a guy you felt was capable of more which calls into question his effort.

D.J. Jones (Ole Miss) 6-0 321 5.10: Decent player who clogs the lane with a wide body. Swallows up running backs that come into his space but very limited speed-wise. Will mostly be a run-stopper and nothing else.

Woody Baron Virginia Tech) 6-1 280 5.11: Massive-sized athlete who has some agility as well. Plays with a nasty streak and was a consistent performer throughout his college career in terms of plugging the run game. Can slip the odd gap and put heat on the passer but mostly Baron is all-or-nothing there.

Treyvon Hester (Toledo) 6-3 300 5.09: While not overly big in size, Hester makes up for it in brute strength and tremendous leg drive. Was able to take on two blockers at the small school level so that those behind him can come up and make the play. Speed works well enough in short bursts and Hester can split the gap if given the chance. Could use another 10-15 pounds to help maximize overall solid but unspectacular ability.

Patrick Gamble (Georgia Tech) 6-4 277 5.07: Likely need to move to the outside in a 3-4 to have a chance to stick. Gamble is physically not able to fight through double-teams in the middle given his lack of power and he plays too upright as well. Lacks the first step to be a consistent pass rusher as well. Contributed on special teams which could be his path to an NFL job. Decent run-stopper when not having to fight through double-teams. Likely a free agent add.

Stevie Tu'ikolovatu (Southern Cal) 6-1 320 5.28: Small but stout defensive tackle. Plays with good leverage and base. Wide-bodied defender who helps in the run game. Severely lacking in burst or any type of speed which makes Tu'ikolovatu a one-dimensional player.

Aaron Curry (TCU) 6-2 278 4.98: Picked up 5.5 sacks as a senior and has very impressive speed for a defensive tackle. No doubt Curry took advantage of blockers more focused on Josh Carraway which needs to be factored into his draft outlook. Grades out as a decent enough pass rusher but who relies solely on splitting the gap. Can't win the one-on-one battle very often given the lack of power and leg drive. Pushed out of too many plays which allowed runners to make big gains going through the middle. Could go to the outside in a 3-4 setup.

Matthew Godin (Michigan) 6-5 294 5.12: Tall and lanky senior who picked up just one sack and two tackles for loss in 2016. Very poor production in terms of numbers and Godin's slight frame has a lot to do with it. Doesn't seem to have a position at the NFL level as Godin is too small for the middle and too slow for the outside.

A.J. Wolf (Duke) 6-4 280 4.94: Has good speed and a nice first step but Duke is likely a special teams guy at best for the NFL if he even gets drafted. High-motor kid but he is very lean size-wise and lacking in strength. Doesn't shed blocks in tight and any push he gets is when splitting gaps off the snap.

Ralph Green III (Indiana) 6-4 305 5.14: Just an average player who doesn't jump off the page anywhere. Likely headed for a free agent invite as Green doesn't generate much push in the pocket and instead relies on the play coming to him. Has size but Green doesn't take advantage of it often enough.

THE REST

*Jeremy Faulk (Garden City CC) 6-1 305

Chunky Clements (Illinois) 6-3 304

Joey Ivie (Florida) 6-3 300

B.J. Singleton (Houston) 6-3 312

Grover Stewart (Albany State) 6-4 347

Patrick Ricard (Maine) 6-3 285

Travis Tuiloma (BYU) 6-2 301

Josh Banks (Wake Forest) 6-3 275

Ondre Pipkins (Texas Tech) 6-3 303

Darius Hamilton (Rutgers) 6-2 278

OUTSIDE LINEBACKER

Position Grade: B+

First Round Talent: Tim Williams, Zach Cunningham, Takkarist McKinley

Analysis: Outside linebacker historically is a close second behind defensive end in terms of quality of talent and 2017 is no exception. In actuality, the gap between the two is wider than it has been in awhile.

Tim Williams (Alabama) 6-3 252 4.68: Just a one-year starter for the Tide but it was a terrific one as Williams was a non-stop pass rushing demon in 2016. Racked up 8.5 sacks and 15 tackles for loss while showcasing a very explosive burst off the edge. Has a clear nose for the quarterback as Williams was always in opposing teams' backfields last season. Plays with impressive leg drive and top pass rushing fundamentals. What really stands out is Williams' explosive first step as he seemingly goes from 0-60 in a flash. For all Williams does on the pass rushing side, he pretty much is a one-dimensional player since he has not shown much in the way of a run prevention game. Can be overpowered at the point of attack and Williams doesn't use his hands well both to shed blocks and to knock the football free. Perhaps the most troubling issue is the fact Williams was arrested early last season for carrying a gun without a permit which got him a first half suspension against Kentucky. There is a bit of bust potential here as Williams needs to really bring his pass rushing skills to the pros since he struggles elsewhere.

NFL Comparison: Bruce Irvin

*****Zach Cunningham (Vanderbilt) 603 230 4.74:** While Tim Williams is all speed in terms of making plays, Zach Cunningham centers as more of a power pass rusher. Also unlike Williams, Cunningham uses his long arms very effectively in terms of knocking down passes or stripping runners of the football. Good but not great reaction off the snap, Cunningham excels at fighting through blocks with terrific hand placement and the skills to knock down an opposing lineman's grab. Delivers a strong hit and keeps his stance when in tight. Really needs to get to work on tackling however as Cunningham lunges way too much and doesn't which allowed more than a few runners to slip his grasp.

NFL Comparison: Lorenzo Alexander

Takkarist McKinley (UCLA) 6-2 258 4.62: Impressive pass rushing specialist who ideally works best on the outside in a 3-4 alignment. Constantly disruptive last season as McKinley picked up 10 sacks and 18 tackles for loss. McKinley has incredible explosion off the snap along the lines of Tim Williams and he can close on most runners. Showed how good he uses in hands as McKinley knocked down 6 passes and forced 3 fumbles. Good change-of-direction skills and has a nice swim move. A one-dimensional player as McKinley is a below-average run defender who doesn't shed blocks well. Too often was pushed out of plays due to a lack of upper-body strength and McKinley fails to generate much in terms of a bull rush push.

*T.J. Watt (Wisconsin) 6-4 243 4.74: Yes he is the younger brother of former Badger and NFL Defensive Player of the Year J.J. Watt. The relationship there alone will likely inflate T.J. Watt's draft stock given the genes. As far as his game is concerned, the younger version of Watt is an adept edge rushing outside linebacker who also was an above-average asset in the run-stopping game. While he has nowhere near the natural skills of his brother, T.J. Watt is a solid all-around player who makes the most out of his ability. There is some remaining upside here which should allow Watt to rise among draft boards leading up to the event. While he has impressive strength in his hands and lower body, Watt needs to vary up and expand his pass rushing arsenal. He is a terrific run stopper as Watt gets into running lanes and attacks the carrier. Sometimes Watt gets too overaggressive and runs past the play and he really struggles badly when asked to drop into coverage.

Haason Reddick (Temple) 6-2 230 4.62: Reddick got after the quarterback at a very consistent level for the Owls but a lack of size will inhibit him when making the jump to the NFL. Picked up 9.5 sacks in 2016 to go along with 21.5 tackles for loss. Clearly has a nose for the quarterback and Reddick has as good a burst as you can get from an edge rusher. Very quick off the snap and can close in a hurry. Disrupts the running game when Reddick can use his speed to get into the pocket but otherwise he is just average there. Will struggle in tight and when locked up as Reddick is terribly slight physically.

Ryan Anderson (Alabama) 6-2 253 4.78: Anderson played opposite Tim Williams as part of the ferocious Tide linebacker unit. Likely inflated his numbers a bit with Williams on the other side but Anderson has good pass rushing chops himself. Not exceptionally quick, Anderson generates his heat through power and a very good bull rush. Needs work stopping the run as Williams does as well. Has a checkered past since Anderson was arrested in 2015 for domestic violence and criminal mischief; issues that will not play well considering how much trouble the league has had on that front lately.

*Alex Anzalone (Florida) 6-2 241 4.70: Suffered a broken arm that ended his 2016 season early. Powerful outside linebacker who can shed blocks and fight his way up the field with impressive hand skills. While he has good but not great speed off the snap, Anzalone was lauded for his work ethic. He is more of a straight-line rusher instead of coming off the edge since Anzalone doesn't have much in the way of explosive speed.

Duke Riley (LSU) 6-0 227 4.56: Leader among the always stalwart Tigers defense. While clearly very small for the linebacker position, Riley showed in 2016 that he had the natural strength to break away from blockers and use his above-average speed to close on the runner or quarterback. Has blazing speed for an outside linebacker as Riley can get the edge in a flash off the snap. Slips gaps nicely and possesses a swim move to dart around tackles. Risks getting pushed out of plays completely given the lack of weight however which needs to be fixed at the NFL level.

*Elijah Lee (Kansas State) 6-3 220 4.76: Not a huge numbers linebacker but Lee has exceptional hands that allowed him to pick up a very high number of interceptions in college. Good tackler who diagnoses the play quickly and gets into position to make an impact but Lee is just an average pass rusher since he doesn't have much quickness. Lee does also has to add some weight and quickly or else he is going to have a very rough go of it in the pros.

Devonte Fields (Louisville) 6-3 242 4.65: Speedy pass rushing outside linebacker, this transfer from TCU has quite a bit of off-the-field concerns to address. Exploded onto the collegiate scene as a freshman when Fields picked up 10 sacks but then the trouble started. Fields missed the next two seasons with some serious injuries and that is another red flag box that he checks. On skills alone, Fields grades out as an impressive speed rusher who can quickly get the edge. Has also shows a very high motor and decent array of moves out of his stance. Non-existent in the run stopping game however and Fields struggles when in tight. Lacks power in all facets of his game and overall is a risk given troubles outside of the field.

Vince Biegel (Wisconsin) 6-4 245 4.74: Consistent and rock solid outside linebacker for the Badgers. Biegel was generally a 5-8 sack guy during his collegiate career and was known for getting the most out of his limited ability.

Interesting combination physically as Biegel is tall for a 'backer but light in his frame. Generates some pass rush through a nice collection of moves and counter moves but Biegel struggles to maintain positioning when engaged with a blocker. Has long arms that are a help in run defense but Biegel needs to work on better getting himself free from in tight. Good player but the ceiling really doesn't go very high.

Carroll Phillips (Illinois) 6-3 240 4.62: Another kid who has serious talent but who will slide in the draft due to off-the-field trouble. Extremely productive pass rusher on the outside as Phillips put up 9 sacks and 20 tackles for loss in 2016. Phillips is quite adept at using his explosive speed to get a high amount of pressure from the outside but he also can swim underneath and slip the gap as well. Packs a punch when laying the wood on a ball-carrier but Phillip also seems uninterested at times in terms of stopping the run. He doesn't show good awareness on that side of the game when it comes to diagnosing plays and also figuring out where to go. Relies solely on athleticism to make an impact and Phillips overall may not offer enough to ignore the off-the-field trouble.

Ejuan Price (Pittsburgh) 5-11 250 4.90: Not sure Price has a firm position as he is a bit in-between as an end or an outside linebacker. Price has a very small frame and a lack of reach which will hurt him at the point of attack. Now on the plus side, Price clearly showed an ability to generate a rush as the 13 sacks he picked up last season are impressive no matter the level. Price is a medical red flag though as he missed both the 2012 and 2014 seasons with injury.

Dylan Donahue (West Georgia) 6-3 240 4.73: Very tough finding good film on Donahue given the very small school background at West Georgia but the kid set all sorts of sack records at his alma mater. What will get Donahue a long look is the fact he runs very well and gets off the snap with nice explosion. He needs to develop as a pure pass rushing end or outside linebacker though since Donahue is a string bean physically and won't have much success dealing with the size of offensive linemen.

Tyus Bowser (Houston) 6-2 240 4.67: Registered 7.5 sacks last season despite missing four games with injury. Highly effective pass rusher who has a non-stop motor. Always seems to be moving forward as Bowser has speed to get to the edge and also the hand-to-hand combat skills to shed blocks in tight. While Bowser does a nice job diagnosing plays, his tackling is shoddy as he comes in too high and doesn't wrap properly. Likely a rotational pass rusher in the NFL.

Dylan Cole (Missouri State) 6-0 240 4.68: Cole put himself into America's consciousness with viral YouTube videos showing his massive bench-pressing power. Cole benched 225 pounds (which is the standard Combine total) 36 times which was a great way of gaining notice since he comes from a small school program. Clearly Cole has the power and strength to shed blocks and get into an opposing teams' backfield. Speed numbers are also quite attractive as well which will make Cole one of the more sought-after late round picks.

Matt Milano (Boston College) 6-0 221: Fast and disruptive linebacker who obviously has the smarts down pat being from B.C. There is a chance Milano could be converted to safety as he runs very well and has impressive change-of-direction ability. Can pack a bit of a punch as well when delivering a hit. Coverage skills are decent but coming up to stop the run a chore given the fact Milano is easily overpowered.

Tashawn Bower (LSU) 6-4 242 4.73: Bower has a nice combination of power and size. Agility is only average as Bower is pretty much a north-south rusher who can't consistently get the edge. Reaction time off the snap is also a bit on the slow side. Pad level needs to be lower to gain leverage but Bower has the long arms and wingspan to be an asset in stopping the run. Could help on special teams.

Jalen Reeves-Maybin (Tennessee) 6-0 230 4.60: Senior campaign was almost a complete washout after Reeves-Maybin suffered a serious shoulder injury last September. Prior to the injury, Reeves-Maybin was a sideline-to-sideline linebacker who graded out as a very effective run stopper. Speed is terrific and Reeves-Maybin can close on the quarterback or runner rapidly. Has little in the way of a secondary move when rushing the passer so Reeves-Maybin needs to rely almost exclusively on his running ability to make plays.

Steven Taylor (Houston) 6-1 225 4.77: Versatile linebacker who helps across the board without excelling in any one area. Does a nice job getting push up the field and also can be trusted to go out in pass coverage. Lacks burst and pure speed to make plays all over the field but takes care of what is in his radius.

James Onwualu (Notre Dame) 6-1 232 4.72: Athletic and versatile, Onwualu can help on special teams early on as he gets up to speed on being a pro linebacker. Severely lacking in size and strength, Onwualu's speed is his primary asset in terms of making plays. Onwualu does generates some heat on the QB with a good first step and spin move and if he puts on some weight, the kid has a chance to overachieve.

Calvin Munson (San Diego State) 6-1 245 4.78: Was drafted by the St. Louis Cardinals out of high school as Munson is a tremendous athlete who has excelled in two sports. Can throw 93-mph but decided he wanted to play for the Aztecs instead of pursuing a pro baseball career. Again Munson is a fluid athlete who makes plays all over the field with his above-average speed and change-of-direction skills. Delivers a hard hit and leaves it all out on the field. Is overall more of a run stopper then a pass rusher since Munson doesn't have the pure strength to break free of many blockers in tight.

Brandon Bell (Penn State) 6-1 233 4.75: Missed four games as a senior with injury but in between registered 3 sacks and 6.5 tackles for loss. It was an underwhelming overall performance though and Bell is likely headed for special teams duty or a backup linebacker spot if he gets drafted. Not much of an impact player as Bell is just an average run defender and a below-average pass rusher given his mediocre athletic ability.

Jimmie Gilbert (Colorado) 6-4 230 4.74: Tall and lanky speedster who played very well as an edge rusher in Colorado's 3-4 system in 2016. Registered 9 sacks and was a real handful when rushing the passer. Gilbert is a heck of an athlete for his height and uses his burst to split gaps or go wide. Changes direction well and can drop into coverage if need be. Lacks functional strength and won't make any type of positive impact stopping the run.

Praise Martin-Oguike (Temple) 6-1 255 4.76: Short and squatty player who gets push through a decent bull rush and fighting through blocks with force. Martin-Oguike has a slow release off the snap and is wildly inconsistent when coming off the edge as he has just mediocre athleticism.

Psalm Wooching (Washington) 6-3 231 4.76: Possesses good height and thump at the point of attack. Combines good hand placement and leg drive to push up the field and make plays in the run game. Limited athletically and gets most of his sacks through force. Likely a free agent signing.

Keenan Gilchrist (Appalachian State) 6-2 225 4.77: Another small school product who opened some eyes with good sack totals and a knack for causing disruption in the opposing team's backfield. Extremely slight frame needs quite a bit of added weight and strength. Can't hold his ground in tight and Gilchrist's performance in the run game was average at best.

THE REST

Samson Ebukam (Eastern Washington) 6-1 238

Pita Taumopenu (Utah) 6-1 242

Michael Hutchings (Southern Cal) 6-1 218

Jordan Burton (Oklahoma State) 6-2 215

Praise Martin-Oguike (Temple) 6-1 255

Gary Thompson (Marshall) 6-1 243

Paul Magloire Jr. (Arizona) 6-0 225

Otha Peters (UL Lafayette) 6-1 228

Jamal Marcus (Akron) 6-1 240

Joshua Polsley (Ball State) 6-1 252

INSIDE LINEBACKER

Position Grade: C+

First Round Talent: Reuben Foster, Raekwon McMillan

Analysis: This is perhaps the most top-heavy position in the draft as once Reuben Foster and Raekwon McMillan go off the board, the drop is steep.

Reuben Foster (Alabama) 6-1 244 4.73: The heart-and-soul of the dominant Alabama Crimson Tide defense in 2016, middle linebacker Reuben Foster is a top-tier talent no matter the position. Foster is a tremendous athlete who has sideline-to-sideline speed to make plays all over the field and is excellent at quickly diagnosing the play and putting himself in position to make the tackle. Racked up 115 tackles, 13 tackles for loss, and five sacks as a senior. Packs a real punch physically and will make players think twice before coming into his space. Gets exposed in pass coverage though as Foster can be too aggressive for his own good and fall prey to pump fakes. While the speed is excellent, Foster loses a step when forced to suddenly change direction which gets him beat him the passing game. Overall this is a top fifteen pick as Foster has the speed and diagnosing skills to be a perennial 100-tackle middle linebacker as soon as his rookie campaign.

NFL COMPARISON: C.J. Mosley

*Raekwon McMillan (Ohio State) 6-2 240 4.70: Physical and powerful middle linebacker who is a terrific run defender. Has the fluidity and speed to get to the ball carrier and make the stop. Plays with a mean streak and can fight free from blocks with impressive strength and leg drive. Struggles badly in pass coverage however and McMillan looks to bring down the runner too often with hitting and not proper tackling technique. Reaches too much and doesn't always wrap up properly as well. There are some whispers McMillan is a product of a strong overall Buckeyes defense.

Jarrad Davis (Florida) 6-1 238 4.74: Has experience both playing in the middle and the outside. Numbers were down as a senior and overall his season was a disappointment as Lee also missed three games with injury. Davis' strength lies in stopping the run as he shows an aptitude to read the play as it unfolds and then go up to deliver big hits. He also shows impressive burst and acceleration to get into the backfield as well. Unlike Raekwon McMillan and Reuben Foster, Davis is not a negative in pass defense. The problems here reside in Davis' struggles in tight and getting through blocks. Has a very slight frame that can easily be pushed aside. Finesse player at a position that requires physicality.

*Anthony Walker Jr. (Northwestern) 6-1 235 4.69: Took some heat for putting on 20 pounds entering into the 2016 season and many felt the added heft derailed Walker's numbers. While he still picked up 105 tackles, Walker Jr. was considered a bit of a letdown on the Northwestern defense. Weight gain or not, Walker Jr. was known for instant acceleration off the snap and the ability to use his well above-average speed to get into an opposing team's backfield to create havoc. Walker Jr. reads the play nicely and can get the edge if need be but he struggles badly to get off blocks when in tight. The added weight was supposed to address this but it wound up costing Walker Jr. his speed last season. Could be more of a dreaded tweener athletically.

Kendell Beckwith (LSU) 6-2 252 4.75: While a clear liability in pass coverage, Beckwith proved himself to be a very good run stopper on the LSU defense. Very good and consistent tackler who made most of the plays in his zone but Beckwith doesn't have the pure speed to be a sideline-to-sideline player. Has the thump to put a hurt on the runner and be somewhat intimidating. He also can be a bit of an injury risk as Beckwith dealt with missed games in college due to some health setbacks .

Connor Harris (Lindenwood) 5-11 243 4.75: While Harris comes from a D-II program, he has the eye-opening distinction of being the all-time tackling leader in college football history. Classic overachieving kid who doesn't possess impressive strength or speed but who was always in position to make the play. Excellent in run support and also a help while in pass coverage. Has six career interceptions and disengages blocks very well which is a plus. Had a serious shoulder injury that required surgery after Harris tore 3 ligaments in the joint. Will struggle at the NFL level when it comes to keeping up with the more speedy receivers in pass coverage as Harris doesn't have good change-of-direction speed and falls prey to pump fakes. Slight frame that may not be able to withstand the rigors of dealing with opposing blockers.

Marquel Lee (Wake Forest) 6-3 240 4.73: Durable and very experienced linebacker who was fourth in the ACC in tackles with 60 last season. That statistic indicates that Lee is a very good run stopper who employs a textbook tackling technique. Lee is a bit taller than you would like from a middle linebacker as he lacks fluidity in his movements carrying that type of frame. Not a true sideline-to-sideline guy as well since Lee lacks pure speed but he makes up for it with a hard-charging approach.

Jayon Brown (UCLA) 5-11 220 4.74: Tackling machine who racked up 119 stops in 2016. Brown has very good instincts and the ability to find the runner and come up to make the stop. Impresses with fluid change-of-direction skill and can split blockers to disrupt the play. Undersized player for the middle as Brown is just 220 pounds and really needs to bulk up. Brown does risk getting blown out of a high number of plays at the NFL level given lack of size. Productive player for the Bruins overall and seems to be one of those guys who always puts in a good day's work.

Riley Bullough (Michigan State) 6-1 227 4.82: Solid and consistent run defender for the Spartans but Bullough lacks the athletic ability to be much more than a backup at the NFL level. Doesn't generate pass rushing heat and is pretty much a stationary linebacker who makes the plays that come into his area code.

Ben Boulware (Clemson) 6-0 235 4.76: Gets a boost from being a productive player on the championship-winning Clemson Tigers defense but overall Boulware doesn't have the look of an NFL starter given his athletic and size limitations. Boulware gets by on guile and smarts but that only goes so far when making the jump to the pros. A liability in pass coverage, Boulware's positives center on good tackling technique that he uses to help in the run game.

Ben Gedeon (Michigan) 6-2 247 4.85: Lacks experience as Gedeon is just a one-year starter and he wasn't considered a prime player on the stout Michigan defense. Did have a solid senior campaign with 106 tackles and 15.5 tackles for loss but Gedeon has athletic limitations that will get taken advantage of in terms of pass coverage and making plays out of his defensive zone.

Eric Wilson (Cincinnati) 6-1 220 4.68: Impressive run game disrupter in the middle as Wilson combines a high football IQ with decent straight-line speed. Physically just can't hold up in tight against bigger blockers given very small frame and could even be a candidate to move to safety. Can help on special teams which will allow Wilson to get on the field early in his career as he works on his overall game.

Hardy Nickerson (Illinois) 6-0 230 4.70: Yes he is the son of the longtime NFL linebacker by the same name. Transferred to Illinois to play for his father as a senior and learned under the guidance of former NFL head coach Lovie Smith.

Clearly has the genes and the tutelage down pat given the professional guidance but overall Nickerson is an average prospect who will likely only get drafted very late given his name. On the field, Nickerson has good range and can use his decent speed to make stops all over the field. Unfortunately Nickerson lacks power and gets eliminated from plays all too often. Struggles to anchor in tight and is slow to react to the play off the snap but Nickerson can help on special teams right away which will help his standing.

Jordan Evans (Oklahoma) 6-2 235 4.82: Evans gets his hands on the football as he picked up a high amount of pass deflections and even added some picks for the Sooners. Overall Evans is a marginal prospect who severely lacks explosion and speed which limits his impact. Range is mediocre and Evans is mostly a backup option if he does get drafted once the late rounds arrive.

THE REST

Harvey Langi (BYU) 6-2 252

Keith Kelsey (Louisville) 6-0 236

Keith Brown (Western Kentucky) 6-0 240

Brooks Ellis (Arkansas) 6-2 245

Blair Brown (Ohio) 5-11 234

Kevin Davis (Colorado State) 6-1 237

Tanner Vallejo (Boise State) 6-1 233

Tim Kimbrough (Georgia) 6-0 226

Jordan Herdman (Simon Fraser) 5-11 238

Trevon Johnson (Weber State) 6-0 231

STRONG SAFETY

Position Grade: B

First Round Talent: Jamal Adams, Jabril Peppers

Analysis: There are two supreme talents here in Jamal Adams and Jabril Peppers but both safety spots remain quite barren.

*Jamal Adams (LSU) 6-1 211 4.50: It is very rare to see a safety get picked among the top 15 players in a given NFL draft but it will happen in 2017 when it comes to LSU's hard-hitting Jamal Adams. Adams is about as complete a safety prospect as you can find as he explodes off the snap and comes up rapidly to make stops. Eagerly takes on blockers and has the burst to slip past if need be. Open-field tackling is tremendous and completely textbook. Delivers a big hit to unsuspecting ball-carriers and also has fluid change-of-direction skills to recover if he makes a rare misstep. Excellent cover man as well since Adams anticipates throws and routes. About the only knock here is that Adams tends to bite on fakes and misdirection. Otherwise he is a star player who will make a great first round pick for someone.

NFL Comparison: Tyrann Mathieu

*Jabril Peppers (Michigan) 6-0 205 4.40: My goodness this kid can run. Peppers has truly elite burst and acceleration which gives him the ability to run with any receiver and also serve as a prime run stopper given the top-notch range he possesses. Has the power in his legs to lay the wood as well and Peppers is far from a finesse defender. Extremely versatile as Peppers was one of the best punt returners in the nation in 2016 and also carried the ball 17 times for 150 yards and 3 touchdowns on offense. Despite the uncanny athleticism, Peppers is not a great cover guy as he had some rough games on that side of things last season and he also doesn't get his hands on the football much which could call into question the instincts.

NFL Comparison: Eric Berry

Justin Evans (Texas A@M) 6-0 200 4.58: Sound and physical safety, Justin Evans is a notch or two below Jamal Adams and Jabril Peppers in terms of overall ability. Lacks the speed and pure athleticism of those two but Evans also is a very good pass coverage guy and has the nose to come up and make a high level of stops in the run game. Not overly flashy but Evans gets the job done on a consistent basis and there is something to be said for this.

Eddie Jackson (Alabama) 6-0 194 4.59: Saw his senior season end after eight games with a broken leg. Prior to this bit of misfortune, Jackson was a dependable producer for the Crimson Tide both at safety and in the return game. While not a burner, Jackson returned two punts for scores and has the cutting ability to make plays there. Made the move from safety to cornerback in 2015. Jackson is a very good cover guy but his lack of size and weight cause issues when dealing with bigger wideouts. Tends to also get pushed around a bit when coming up to stop the run but no one questions the effort.

Josh Harvey-Clemons (Louisville) 6-4 228 4.65: Got invited to the Senior Bowl but Harvey-Clemons had just an average senior campaign. While he is a very physical and hard-hitting safety, Harvey-Clemons never really had any "wow" games that made one take notice. Has to answer for being dismissed from Georgia in 2014 over repeated off-the-field issues and team violations. Average ability and off-the-field trouble is not a very good recipe for being drafted high.

Jadar Johnson (Clemson) 6-0 210 4.65: Here is a classic overachiever for you. Johnson did his part on the championship-winning Tigers defense as he showed excellent instincts and the ability to find the football which overcame a lack of athleticism. Diagnoses plays rapidly and can fight through blocks with good power and leg drive. While a good hitter, Johnson has some clear struggles while in pass defense. He doesn't change direction well on the fly and is susceptible to quickly falling behind speedy wideouts.

Obi Melifonwu (UCONN) 6-3 216 4.53: Rising very quickly among draft boards as NFL personnel executives get a longer look at this rare physical and athletic specimen. Melifonwu can really run for a man who is 6-3 but he also packs a punch in terms of delivering monster hits in the secondary. While the natural ability is clearly there, Melifonwu doesn't always put it to good use and his instincts are lacking. Got beat in pass coverage too often and seemed a bit hesitant off the snap of where to go. A work in progress but boy that athleticism is something.

Tedric Thompson (Colorado) 6-0 205 4.56: Nice and athletic safety who relished delivering big hits. Shows a willingness to get his hands dirty and engage blockers. Can go up and get the football with excellent leaping skills and deflects a high number of passes. Speed is good but not great and Thompson's range is limited as a result. Too aggressive at times to the point of whiffing on plays. A bit reckless which leads to penalties and missed assignments.

*Montae Nicholson (Michigan State) 6-1 219 4.60: Early entrant safety who should have stayed in school for another year as Nicholson is not going to be much more than a late round pick. While his overall numbers are decent, Nicholson has some major issues in pass coverage. Often getting beat deep, Nicholson needs to do a better job reading the quarterback while also focusing on his man and he tends to lose a step when having to change direction. Not a great tackle either as Nicholson goes in too high and allows the runner to slip his grasp. What Nicholson does do well is lay the wood as a ferocious hitter who will make receivers think twice about going over the middle. Nicholson can also help on special teams with his very good straight-line speed.

Xavier Woods (Louisiana Tech) 5-11 219 4.58: This is one kid who coaches will love. Was talked about as a leader on the Louisiana Tech defense and Woods possesses intriguing late round talent in both facets of the defensive game. While Woods has a slight build, he proved to be a very effective player out in pass defense. Woods successfully makes plays on the ball with good anticipation and does a nice job warding off his opponent. Comes up to make stops in the run game as well but Woods does struggle at times to get through blocks.

Dallas Lloyd (Stanford) 6-2 213 4.64: Lloyd is a hard-hitting safety who relishes getting involved in the rough stuff. Comes off the snap quickly and is eager to lay a hit on someone. Has limitations in terms of a lack of speed which is seen in Lloyd's poor pass coverage skills. Can take your head off going over the middle however and being a physical presence with be Lloyd's calling card.

Weston Steelhammer (Air Force) 6-1 200 4.59: Could be the only service academy player drafted. Picked up 80 tackles and 5 interceptions as a senior and shows very impressive ball skills in pass coverage. Also an accomplished baseball player who could get a look in the MLB Draft as well. Leader and highly intelligent, Steelhammer's determination alone could very well get him a late round chance.

D'Nerius Antoine (Southern Mississippi) 5-11 215 4.58: While not an overly impressive athlete, Antoine is a good hitter who makes plays stopping the run. Struggles to maintain pass coverage down the field as Antoine lacks acceleration and decent change-of-direction ability. Tackling could use some shoring up as well.

Nathan Gerry (Nebraska) 4.75: Very slow of foot for a safety but Gerry has a clear nose for the football as he deflected 8 passes and picked off four throws in 2016. Smart and tough player who maximizes his ability despite not having much in the way of speed.

Shalom Luani (Washington State) 6-0 198 4.57: First Cougars defensive back to be named All-Pac-12 First-Team since 2013. Got his hands on a ton of balls as Luani grabbed 4 interceptions and knocked down 6 other throws. Instinctive player who all too often makes the correct read and puts himself in position to make plays. A bit of a string bean physically, Luani needs to add bulk to boost his lacking run support ability.

Orion Stewart (Baylor) 6-1 205 4.60: A bit of a checkered past as Stewart was handed a team suspension in 2015 and also missed games that year with injury. Rebounded with a productive senior campaign where Stewart picked up 5 picks and 6 passes defended. Possesses good height and hips that are conducive for being a good pass coverage guy but Stewart is not much of a hitter. Stewart misses too many tackles and is hesitant to engage in contact.

Dante Barnett (Kansas State) 6-0 193: Tough and very experienced player for K-State. Barnett was a team captain the last two years and was a big-hitting safety who left it all on the field. While the desire was always there, Barnett is limited athletically as he lacks fluidity and the smooth hip movement to help in pass defense. Comes up to stop the run with aggressiveness and tackling grades our as generally solid. Character kid who should be given a shot.

THE REST

Dymonte Thomas (Michigan) 5-11 195

Nate Gerry (Nebraska) 6-2 214

Shalom Luani (Washington State) 6-0 198

Leon McQuay III (Southern Cal) 6-1 192

Donald Payne (Stetson) 5-11 195

Damarius Travis (Minnesota) 6-0 211

Tony Conner (Ole Miss) 6-0 225

Damarlay Drew (California) 5-11 202

Money Hunter (Arkansas State) 6-1 210

Randall Goforth (UCLA) 5-11 185

FREE SAFETY

Position Grade: B-

First Round Talent: Malik Hooker

Analysis: Led by the top five overall talent that is Malik Hooker, free safety has some prospects that could go in Rounds 2-3 behind the Ohio State product.

*Malik Hooker (Ohio State) 6-2 205 4.47: Will join Jamal Adams as potential top ten picks in the 2017 NFL Draft. You can make the argument that Hooker was one of the most dominant players overall in college football last season as he racked up 74 tackles (5.5 for loss), 4 passes batted down, and a massive 7 interceptions. Three of those picks were returned for scores which speaks to the top-notch athleticism Hooker possesses. Love the ball skills here which are as impressive as any safety to come out since Sean Taylor. Hooker is adept at pass coverage; showing the extreme ability to change direction and not lose a step. He can also close in a flash once the pass is in the air and shows the aggressiveness to come up and stop the run. Finally Hooker did bite on a few play fakes and tackling may be the one clear area he needs to improve upon.

NFL Comparison: Earl Thomas

*Budda Baker (Washington) 5-10 192 4.65: While Baker is quite lanky and lacking in pure strength, the Washington junior has tremendous range to make plays all over the field. Textbook tackler in the run-stopping game and has the quickness and agility to be an asset in pass defense. Like with Malik Hooker, Baker needs to get to work on shoring up his tackling.

Marcus Williams (Utah) 6-1 195 4.55: Tall and rangy safety who has the speed to cover a lot of ground. Doesn't pack much of a punch as Williams has a very slight build but he stays low when making the tackle. Picked off five passes and knocked down five others last season as a junior which shows Williams has some nice coverage ability.

Desmond King (Iowa) 5-10 203 4.53: You can make the argument that Desmond King is one of the more underrated players in the draft. King can go up and get the football with his tremendous vertical leaping ability and he also has the fluidity to stay with most receivers in one-on-one coverage. Reads the quarterback nicely and gets into many passing lanes as well. Makes textbook tackles as well and King is a tough kid who can deliver a decent hit. Pure speed is not as good as you would like though which King could get away with in college. He may have issues against speedy deep threats in the pros as a result and King's range is not ideal.

Marcus Maye (Florida) 5-11 216 4.63: Suffered a season-ending broken arm but was expected to be fully healed for the Senior Bowl. Prior to the injury, Maye was cementing his status as an athletic safety that had very good range to make stops both in the run game and in pass defense. May was an inconsistent cover guy though as he often loses track of the football and gave up way too many deep completions. Decent run-stopper for a guy with modest size but Maye can be a bit too hit-or-miss overall as a prospect.

*Josh Jones (N.C. State) 6-2 215 4.56: It is very rare for a safety to rack up over 100 tackles but that is just what Jones did in 2016 by picking up 109 stops. That suggests Jones has the instincts and know-how to disrupt plays and collect tackles. This skill works nicely in the run game but Jones was exposed when out in pass protection. While Jones is athletic, he loses track of the football when looking back at the QB and he often gets out-muscled when in tight.

Lorenzo Jerome (St. Francis Pa.) 5-11 195 4.60: The very small-school product that is Lorenzo Jerome is gaining some attention due to his very intriguing ball skills. Picked up a slew of interceptions and deflected passes while in college and his pass coverage ability was terrific. With swivel hips and good change-of-direction skills, Jerome can stay with most wideouts down the field. Where he will have to really improve is stopping the run. Jerome needs to gain strength and add weight to really give himself a chance but the ability is apparent.

Rayshawn Jenkins (Miami Fla.) 6-1 208 4.67: Came back from an injury-marred junior campaign to post an effective senior season for the Hurricanes that earned him an invite to the Senior Bowl Jenkins is a very physical and hard-hitting safety who fights through traffic to make stops. A bit slow of foot, Jenkins has trouble staying with receivers deep and he tends to also bite on pump fakes.

John Johnson (Boston College) 6-1 202 4.62: Like the ball skills here as Johnson picked up 77 tackles, 9 passes broken up, and 3 picks as a senior. Johnson does a nice job breaking down plays and reading the quarterback which helps him make up for speed shortcomings. He could use some more heft on his frame which would help Johnson fight through blocks better and contribute some more in stopping the run.

Jordan Sterns (Oklahoma State) 6-0 200 4.55: Compiled the most tackles of any defensive back in the conference in 2016 as Sterns picked up 96 tackles. Sterns looks like a mid-to-late-round gem who is always around the football and who also makes textbook tackles when in position to make the play. You can't teach the instincts that Sterns possesses and that alone will gain notice. While he is not a big hitter, Sterns doesn't mind mixing things up. Has the speed to work well in pass defense but overall coverage skills are just average.

Jonathan Ford (Auburn) 6-0 203 4.60: Could help right away as a kick returner as Ford learns the nuances of the pro game. Productive but not impactful safety, Ford left you wanting more. Has the speed to make plays all over the field but tackling numbers inconsistent. Good hitter but Ford gets in trouble against stronger receivers.

Fish Smithson (Kansas) 5-11 201 4.63: Love this kid. While not many are talking about him, the Jayhawks' Fish Smithson should be moving up boards soon when his tape circulates more leading up to the draft. Racked up a very impressive 93 tackles and 4 interceptions as a senior and graded out as above-average both in stopping the run and when out in pass coverage. Smithson has smooth acceleration that allows him to have good range and also to close in on passes. A fluid athlete who gets his hands on the football, Smithson has issues with his lack of size and strength. Won't be able to win many one-on-one battles against the bigger-type wideouts in today's NFL and Smithson looks to tackle more than lay a hit.

David Jones (Richmond) 6-2 210 4.53: Likely to draw a free agent invite due to the fact Jones was a ball-hawking safety who picked off a slew of passes in college. Was dominant at times at the small-school level as Jones had his way while in pass coverage and also showed a proclivity to come up and make the stop in the run game. Decent size and strength combination a plus. Overall Jones is raw in terms of quality of competition and the learning curve will be sharp. Needs to learn how to use his height better in walling off receivers and Jones has to work on his tackling technique.

Ahmad Thomas (Oklahoma) 6-0 215 4.67: Very hard-hitting safety who goes all out to put a receiver on the mat. A bit too reckless at times, Thomas leaves himself open for penalties and deep completions. Excellent at fighting through blocks to disrupt the play and physical enough to hold his ground in pass coverage. Doesn't possess good speed though and so Thomas had his difficulties keeping receivers in check.

Delano Hill (Michigan) 6-0 215 4.59: Has forced a bunch of fumbles and picked off a decent number of passes during his collegiate days. Hill gets himself into proper position to get his hands on the football and has good anticipatory skills. Lacks overall agility however as Hill loses his man in coverage when the play goes deep. He also has a tendency to lose a step or two when forced to change direction during any given pattern. Could catch on as a free agent.

THE REST

Chuck Clark (Virginia Tech) 6-0 204

Mike Tyson (Cincinnati) 6-1 198

Maurice Smith (Georgia) 5-11 196

Casey DeAndrade (New Hampshire) 5-11 216

Kai Nacua (BYU) 6-1 216

Zach Edwards (Cincinnati) 5-11 200

Demetrious Cox (Michigan State) 6-0 197

Kivon Coman (Mississippi State) 6-2 196

Ryan Janvion (Wake Forest) 5-11 190

Rickey Jefferson (LSU) 5-11 206

CORNERBACK

Position Grade: A

First Round Talent: Teez Tabor, Marlon Humphrey, Marshon Lattimore, Sidney Jones, Cordrea Tankersley, Gareon Conley

Analysis: The 2017 cornerback class takes a seat behind only the defensive ends when it comes to top-tier talent. The depth here is arguably deeper than their pass rushing brethren as well but the ends still edge them out for the top spot.

*Marshon Lattimore (Ohio State) 6-0 192 4.50: Has the coverage skills to be yet another first-round cornerback. Lattimore can run with most receivers and he has very fluid hips and change-of-direction ability that allows him to stick tightly in coverage. Possesses a great set of hands that can easily pick off the football and Lattimore is also quite adept at closing ground once the pass is in the air. Leaves himself open to deep completion due to a tendency to bite on fakes however. Lattimore also is not overly physical and cedes some ground when jammed off the line. Has a long history of hamstring trouble which required a surgery.

NFL Comparison: Joe Haden

*Marlon Humphrey (Alabama) 6-1 248 4.48: Tremendous cover corner who combines good size/height with impressive speed. Humphrey is constantly attaching himself to the hip of the receiver and constantly fighting for position. Unlike Teez Tabor, Humphrey doesn't always play the ball well when it is in his radius and he has some issues with being beat over the top. Was a five-star recruit when first arriving in Alabama so the pedigree is huge. Love the long arms which Humphrey uses to engulf receivers and he also is physical at the point of attack in showing a nice jam. Can go up and get the football in jump-ball situations. Reads the quarterback nicely and he also is a very durable player. Struggles some when forced to change direction quickly and Humphrey can be prone to taking penalties in grabbing hold too often.

NFL COMPARISON: Patrick Peterson

*Teez Tabor (Florida) 6-0 201 4.49: Textbook cover guy as Tabor has tremendous fluidity and change-of-direction skills. Can close quickly on a receiver once the throw is in the air and Tabor is excellent at looking back at the quarterback but still being able to stick with his man. Has the leaping ability to go up and get the football and Tabor really impresses with his hands in breaking up throws. A bit of a gambler however as Tabor likes to go for the big play but that leaves him vulnerable to deep completions. Speed is very good but not explosive. Loses himself when trying to diagnose and stop running plays. Perhaps the biggest issue is the fact Tabor got himself suspended twice during his Gators tenure. In 2015 it was for refusing to take a drug test and then popping off in social media about it and last season it was for getting into a fight with a teammate.

NFL Comparison: DeAngelo Hall

***Sidney Jones (Washington) 6-0 181 4.52:** Lock-down corner who plays a finesse game. While Jones is far from physical in coverage, he sticks to his man all over the field with a blend of speed and fluid movement. Constantly around the football and Jones has excellent hand skills to knock down throws or make the interception. Keeps himself under control which further allows him to make plays on the ball. Where Jones is going to have trouble is against the bigger and more physical wideouts. Can be jammed backwards and loses momentum. Missed tackles also a bit of a problem as Jones doesn't have the strength to consistently win battles in tight.

NFL Comparison: Jimmy Smith

Cordrea Tankersley (Clemson) 6-0 200 4.53: Proved himself an NFL prospect when Tankersley held up well in coverage when opposing QB's threw in his direction to avoid NFL pro and former teammate Mackensie Alexander. While not the fastest corner in the world, Tankersley nicely uses his size to gain positioning on receivers and his physical approach resulted in quite a few plays made on the football. Has excellent leaping ability and long arms to maintain control in coverage. Needs to do a better job of looking back at the passer and maintaining his stride. Tankersley also he uses his hands a bit too much to the point he takes penalties.

NFL Comparison: Janoris Jenkins

*Gareon Conley (Ohio State) 6-0 195 4.55: Conley is the other half of the top cornerback pair in the nation at Ohio State along with Marshon Lattimore. More than did the job when quarterbacks threw his way to avoid Lattimore; showing the athleticism to grade out as above-average in pass coverage. Doesn't run nearly as well as his teammate but Conley makes up for it by playing aggressively. Jams the receiver nicely off the snap to gain positioning and fights for the ball when it heads his way. Conley gets beat deep at times due to his lack of acceleration and he struggles to maintain positioning against more shifty receivers.

Tre'Davious White (LSU) 5-11 192 4.53: Big-play cornerback who batted down 14 passes last season and had a pick-six in the Tigers' opener. White was also a very potent return man as well during his collegiate career. What is obvious is that White has tremendous athleticism and speed that helps him immensely against quick wideouts. Where White tends to run into problems is when he matches up against the more physically imposing receivers. Needs to work on jamming better off the snap and fighting for the football in tight. Can run all over the field with any opponent though and White is a scary sight when he does have the football in his hands.

Cameron Sutton (Tennessee) 5-11 186 4.51: Only got into three games as a senior before a broken ankle ended things early for Sutton. Reliable corner who shows a textbook approach which includes effective jams at the line of scrimmage to go with the athleticism to excel in pass coverage. Closes space quickly on a receiver and Sutton has some of the better hand skills of any defensive back in the draft. The downside here is that Sutton is extremely light at 186 pounds and he can be beaten over the top against taller wideouts. Sutton also struggles stopping the run as again his lack of size makes bringing down a runner a chore.

*Quincy Wilson (Florida) 6-0 209 4.50: Excellent body type and physical specimen for an NFL corner. Wilson has terrific straight-line speed but he loses a step or two when forced to stick on deep throws. He comes up like a beast in run support and Wilson is adept at diving low to take out a runner's legs. Wilson plays with swagger and his long arms make it tough on a wideout. Also is somewhat of a hothead who gets in trouble with penalties.

*Adoree' Jackson (Southern Cal) 5-11 185 4.42: Wow what speed and acceleration this kid has. Comes out early off a monster 2016 where Jackson picked off 5 passes, broke up 11 others, and scored four total touchdowns on returns. Electric runner with the ball in his hands, Jackson could be used on offense at the next level while instantly working as a returner. Can clearly run with any receiver but Jackson is a clear notch or two below when it comes to size/strength. Susceptible to being beaten over the top and in particular has trouble with jump balls against taller wideouts around the red zone. Again while Jackson can run like the wind, his coverage skills are not terrific. He also grades out very poorly in stopping the run, with size being another problem there. Could be classified more of an athlete then a ready-made corner.

Jourdan Lewis (Michigan) 5-10 186 4.52: Yet another Wolverines defender who will get drafted, Lewis was a very effective pass defender in the team's secondary.

While short of height, Lewis combined very impressive speed with an athletic fluidity that allowed him to stick tight to his man. Could be moved to slot corner given the clear physical limitations that will expose Lewis at the next level. While no one doubts his coverage ability, Lewis struggles to maintain positioning when grappling with bigger receivers. He also is a below-average run defender who grabs instead of properly wraps up when it comes to tackling.

Rasul Douglas (West Virginia) 6-1 208 4.56: Picked up 8 interceptions in 2016 which shows the ball-hawking ability of Douglas. Contributed on special teams and has a tremendous wingspan to make life difficult on wideouts. While he shows good tackling ability, Douglas is a bit of a finesse guy who shies away from contact in the run game.

Chidobe Awuzie (Colorado) 5-11 205 4.52: Didn't get the attention that many of the corners listed above him received but Awuzie was a dependable four-year starter. He proved himself to be an impressive cover corner who combined that skill with the leaping ability to knock down throws. Awuzie also possesses the speed to close in tight and make plays on the football. The knocks here are that Awuzie is not overly tall and strong and that leads to him giving up completions when facing off against larger wideouts. Can get beaten deep and also struggles to bring down the runner.

*Kevin King (Washington) 6-3 192 4.54: Very rare to see a cornerback this tall. Going with the impressive height, King uses his long arms to gain position and swat away passes. Delivers a good pop on the ball-carrier and has the hand skills to rip the football loose. Shows a textbook tackling technique as well. There is a chance King could be moved to safety as his speed is ordinary for a corner and he loses his man often on deep passes in struggling to match stride. Once he loses a step, King also has issues getting himself back into the play.

*Howard Wilson (Houston) 6-0 185 4.52: Very young and raw corner prospect but Wilson has decent athletic upside which is being taken notice of. Missed all of 2015 with injury and has just a single year of starting experience in college. While not very big physically, Wilson makes up for it with keen anticipation and footwork. Wilson grades out as a solid cover corner but one who is a bit choppy with his hands and gets beaten by double-moves. Needs to add some weight and strength to really elevate his game.

Marquez White (Florida State) 6-0 181 4.58: Tall and lengthy corner who struggled in pass coverage at times during his collegiate career. Not especially fast but White battles receivers with a physical style. Gets himself into position to makes plays on the ball and delivers big hits when needed. Has decent height but vertical agility is not there. Change-of-direction skills are lacking and White could be a nickel corner candidate given his speed issues on the outside.

Damontae Kazee (San Diego State) 5-10 190 4.48: Named Mountain West Defensive Player of the Year in 2016. Smart and technically sound cornerback who makes the most of limited athletic ability. Delivers a good jam at the line of scrimmage and uses his hands to shield a receiver from the ball. Got his hands on a high number of passes and also adept at causing fumbles. Speed issues could get exposed on the outside in the NFL and Kazee lost his man on deeper routes. Gambles way too much which led to big completions while in coverage.

Corn Eider (Miami Fla.) 5-10 180 4.58: Lack of height could push him to a nickel role in the NFL. While Eider is a solid cover man, he also had his share of struggles there. Seemed to alternate good and bad games for the Hurricanes and Eider's issues mostly centered on lack of physicality. Relies too much on finesse and often lets other defenders make the tackle. Can go up and make the interception as Eider has solid leaping ability but his fundamentals need work.

Brendan Langley (Lamar) 6-1 190 4.53: Senior Bowl invitee based on Langley's athleticism and speed. Was a strong returner for Lamer and Langley also has the requisite height and acceleration to eventually turn into a solid defensive back. A clear work in progress given the level he comes from but Langley has intriguing tools to work with. Must fix propensity to gamble which is not so much of a deterrent at the small-school level and tackling is also another weak point.

Channing Stribling (Michigan) 6-1 179 4.52: Very long arm and uncanny height for a corner. A string bean physically though which is seen in Stribling's poor tackling skills and below-average work in stopping the run. Stribling did prove himself as a very good cover man in 2016 however and that is especially impressive when you consider most QB's threw his way in order to avoid fellow corner prospect Jourdan Lewis on the other side. If Stribling puts on some weight, he could really be a fine value selection.

Ahkello Witherspoon (Colorado) 6-2 195 4.59: Earning notice for the uncanny height which gives Witherspoon the advantage of engulfing a wideout in coverage. Witherspoon complements that with the ability to go up and get the football, especially around the red zone. What Witherspoon doesn't have is top-end speed and he gives up too much of a cushion off the snap to prevent deep throws. That results in completions underneath his coverage which could lead to bigger gains. Physical when coming up to stop the run but the instincts on that side of things are not always there.

Aarlon Penton (Missouri) 5-9 180 4.52: Likely needs to grab hold of a nickel corner spot at the pro level as Penton is very short to be on the outside. What Penton lacks in terms of height and strength, he makes up for with speed and the ability to cover all over the field. Doesn't back down from any receiver and Penton has the explosion and acceleration to close ground in a hurry. Won't get into position to make enough stops in the run game to be consistent there and Penton also often gets pushed out of running lanes given the small stature.

Jalen Myrick (Minnesota) 5-10 208 4.58: While he held his own both in stopping the run and in pass coverage, Myrick is nothing more than a late-round pick due to the fact he lacks the athleticism to go any higher. Fights for positioning against receivers and uses long arms to swat down a good number of throws. Struggles to make the interception however as Myrick's hands are not dependable. Throws his weight around in terms of hitting but this also leaves Myrick susceptible to being beaten with a deep throw.

Fabian Moreau (UCLA) 6-0 205 4.56: Underrated cover corner who has a chance to be a late-round steal. Moreau unfortunately had his senior season virtually wiped out due to a painful Lisfranc injury to his foot. Prior to that bit of misfortune, Moreau was trusted in man-to-man coverage and held up very well. Excellent tackler who also can close any open space between he and a receiver quickly. There were some problems with deep balls and losing some physical battles but Moreau surely would be picked higher if not for the injury.

Jeremy Cutrer (Middle Tennessee) 6-1 170 4.49: Extremely slight but very fast and athletic cornerback. Cutrer also possesses the height and length that NFL front offices are on the lookout for. Despite the lack of weight, Cutrer seems to relish coming up and making stops in the run game as he often aims low and delivers a nice hit. Cuter is a confident kid who can be a bit overzealous at times and his gambling style could lead to being burned in coverage. Clearly will need to show he can adequately muscle up against a bigger receiver.

Des Lawrence (North Carolina) 6-0 185 4.55: Decent size and length for a corner but Lawrence struggled mightily in one-on-one coverage for the Tar Heels. Not overly athletic and lacks the speed to cover all over the field. Tough player who likes to get physical but desire and results don't always match up. Likely a nickel guy at the NFL level.

Ezra Robinson (Tennessee State) 6-1 180 4.53: While a small-school prospect, Ezra Robinson has the length and size to at least physically match up against bigger receivers. The speed issue is an obvious one with Robinson though and that is what will determine where his career goes. What really stood out was how Robinson got his hands on a lot of footballs in his collegiate career and he picked off 5 passes as a senior. Decent project.

Ashton Lampkin (Oklahoma State) 6-0 189 4.49: Injury-prone player who missed almost all of 2014 and large chunks of the 2015 seasons. Proved himself to be a solid cover corner who played a physical style. Never backs down when fighting for positioning and was talked about as a leader on the Oklahoma State defense. Shows nice awareness for the football and closes in to make plays quickly. Struggles at times to contain bigger wideouts and Lampkin can get suckered into too many pump fakes.

Treston DeCoud (Oregon State) 6-2 203 4.54: Long and lean corner who has the makeup that NFL execs are looking for to help stop the ever-increasing proliferation of the passing game. While DeCoud won't wow anyone with his speed or athleticism, he is a gamer who plays as a tough corner. DeCoud is not afraid to mix it up with opposing wideouts and his tall frame and long arms are tailor-made for making plays on the ball. He also doesn't seem overly interested in coming up to stop the run, often leaving that chore to the rest of the defense.

Sojourn Shelton (Wisconsin) 5-9 178 4.58: Nickel back corner who had a productive senior campaign that included four picks and 12 passes batted away. There are obvious height and frame concerns here which means Shelton can't work as an outside defender. Run stopping ability is quite shaky but Shelton does a good job staying in an opposing receiver's pocket in taking proper angles. Not especially fleet of foot either for someone his size.

Xavier Coleman (Portland State) 5-11 190 4.53: Garnering seventh-round or free agent attention as Coleman has an attractive combination of size and speed. Was one of the best cover men at his school's level and at the very least Coleman has the athleticism to work with as a project pick. Not overly physical, Coleman relies on fluidity and instincts to make an impact.

Najee Murray (Kent State) 5-9 180 4.48: Another nickel back corner who can help in the return game. Murray's speed is impressive and he uses it to stick close to his man on deep throws. Gives up a lot of short completions due to a tendency to play off his man and avoid jamming which won't be effective given the lack of strength and power.

Jack Tocho (N.C. State) 6-0 200 4.53: There is good height and leaping ability here but Tocho is going to have to settle for being a backup corner and special teams gunner as he was just an average cover guy and run stopper in college. Uses his long arms and active hands to break up passes but Tocho has very limited range on the field.

Josh Thornton (Southern Utah) 5-11 185 4.37: Like with almost all small-school prospects, there has to be something that stands out and in the case of Josh Thornton, it is blazing 4.3 speed. Thornton can make an NFL squad on his return skills alone and there is a place on any team for him when it comes to this type of explosive acceleration. Since Thornton will be able to cover every inch of a field, he is worth schooling in terms of learning the NFL game as a backup initially.

William Likely III (Maryland) 5-7 175 4.46: Will be drafted on the strength of return skills as Likely III was an All-American there for the Terrapins. Shows good balance and acceleration while in pass coverage and Likely has the confidence to challenge any receiver for the football. Willing tackler but Likely has short arms that make him inconsistent there. Utter lack of height means Likely can be picked on over the top and he will struggle jamming receiver off the snap.

Joshua Holsey (Auburn) 5-11 195 4.52: Suffered a torn ACL last September which obliterated Holsey's senior campaign. He was quite an average player previous to the injury as Holsey was just a nickel corner for Auburn and that is where he will have to stick in the NFL if he gets selected.

Greg Mabin (Iowa) 6-1 200 4.54: Rangy and tall corner who relished delivering hard hits. Inconsistent in pass coverage as Mabin lacks change-of-direction skills and closing speed. Likely a rotational player if he makes an NFL roster.

Tony Bridges (Ole Miss) 6-0 185 4.56: Had a horrendous senior season for the Rebels where Bridges wound up being a liability in pass coverage. Light when it comes to weight which doesn't go well with Bridges' good height. Shouldn't get drafted.

Brad Watson (Wake Forest) 6-0 192 4.52: Decent athlete who can help in a nickel package in the NFL. Built solidly and possesses a hard-hitting approach. Runs hot and cold in pass coverage and tackling is an issue.

Tim Harris (Virginia) 6-1 200 4.58: Was an injury-prone player for Virginia and when on the field, Harris didn't distinguish himself as an NFL prospect. Harris got burned on more than a few occasions on deep throws and he also had major problems sticking to speedy wideouts. Gives a nice jam at the line of scrimmage and can come up and help a bit in the run game. Looks like a free agent signing at best.

THE REST

Jeremy Clark (Michigan) 6-3 206

Tolando Cleveland (Mississippi State) 5-11 190

Nate Hariston (Temple) 6-0 192

Shaquil Griffin (UCF) 6-0 198

DeVon Edwards (Duke) 5-8 180

Taylor Reynolds (James Madison) 5-11 195

DJ Dean (Arkansas) 5-11 199

Brandon Wilson (Houston) 5-10 201

Arthur Maulet (Memphis) 5-9 188

2017 NFL DRAFT ROUND 1 LOG

1. Cleveland Browns-

2. San Francisco 49ers-

3. Chicago Bears-

4. Jacksonville Jaguars-

5. Tennessee Titans-

6. New York Jets-

7. Los Angeles Chargers

8. Carolina Panthers-

9. Cincinnati Bengals-

10. Buffalo Bills-

11. New Orleans Saints-

12. Cleveland Browns

13. Arizona Cardinals-

14. Indianapolis Colts-

15. Philadelphia Eagles-

16. Baltimore Ravens-

17. Washington Redskins-

18. Tennessee Titans-

19. Tampa Bay Buccaneers-

20. Denver Broncos-

21. Detroit Lions-

22. Miami Dolphins-

23. New York Giants-

24. Oakland Raiders-

25. Houston Texans-

26. Seattle Seahawks-

27. Kansas City Chiefs-

28. Dallas Cowboys-

29. Green Bay Packers-

30. Pittsburgh Steelers-

31. Atlanta Falcons-

32. New England Patriots-